How to write your first nonfiction book

VINIL RAMDEV

Copyright © 2020 Vinil Ramdev

All rights reserved. This book contains material protected under International and Federal Copyright Laws and Treaties. Any unauthorized reprint or use of this material is prohibited. No part of this publication may be reproduced, distributed or transmitted in any form or by any means, including photocopying, recording, or other electronic or mechanical methods, without the prior written permission of the publisher, except in the case of brief quotations embodied in critical reviews and certain other noncommercial uses permitted by copyright law. For permission requests, write to the publisher, at the address below.

PublishEdge Enterprises Pvt Ltd
19/24, 1st main rd, Jayamahal, Bangalore, Karnataka, 560046 India

Email: contact@publishedge.com

www.publishedge.com

How to write your first nonfiction book by Vinil Ramdev

Print Book ISBN 978-1-953316-00-4

Disclaimer

The author and publisher of this book have used their best efforts in preparing the book. The authors and publishers make no representation or warranties with respect to the accuracy, applicability and the fitness or completeness of this book. They disclaim any warranties (expressed or implied), merchantability, or fitness for any particular purpose. The authors and publishers shall in no event be held liable for any loss or other damages.

Dedicated to all my readers

"The book you actually write is better than the one you dream of writing."
—JEFF GOINS

Contents

Introduction 7

Chapter 1: Why Do You Want to Write a Book? 9

Chapter 2: Types of Nonfiction Books..............................17

Chapter 3: The Most Important Quality for Writing Success.........27

Chapter 4: How to Come up with a Book Title?......................35

Chapter 5: The Book Plan..43

Chapter 6: Plagiarism and Copyrights.............................51

Chapter 7: Storytelling Formulas 59

Chapter 8: Research Methods 71

Chapter 9: The Writing Process 79

Chapter 10: How to Self-Edit?..91

Chapter 11: How to Hire an Editor?...............................101

Chapter 12: Common Grammatical Errors 109

Chapter 13: Miscellaneous Pages in Your Book...........121

Chapter 14: Business Models for Nonfiction Authors.................131

Chapter 15: Options for Non-Writers 141

Closing Thoughts..149

Bibliography 153

Index 157

Introduction

I'LL NEVER FORGET THAT day—it was seven in the morning—and I could see sunlight creeping through my windows. I'd stayed up the entire night, seated at my desk, writing the last few words and putting the final full stop to the completed version of my first non-fiction book. Hitting that 'complete' button on my first book was a feeling that, even now, fills me with pride and satisfaction.

Did you know that, statistically, almost every second person wants to write a book? Yet, less than one percent of the world's population ever finishes the task. So, even if you write just one book in your entire lifetime, you'll be part of a pretty exclusive club.

You see, the choice is yours—you can decide to join the one percent or stick with the 99 percent. Having had the pleasure of being among the one percent, I want to pass that great feeling of accomplishment along to other would-be writers. When I set out to write this book, I had a single purpose—to help you also become part of that exclusive club, and feel the unique satisfaction of hitting 'the end' for the final time on your first ever non-fiction book.

To help you achieve the objective of writing your first book, I've put everything I've learned over the years about becoming a successful author into this guide. Anyone with even middle-school English language skills can write a book if they follow my instructions. Madeleine L'Engle said, "You have to write the book that wants to be written. And if the book will be too difficult for grown-ups, then you write it for children."

I don't know if being a published author will change your life, although it has changed some people's lives. However, it will get some major baggage out of your system and make you feel lighter and ready to move on to your next project—hopefully, another book! Most people think that it takes intelligence to write a book, but that's not true. Discipline is far more valuable in this project, as personal experience has taught me.

I would like to dedicate this book to the thousands of readers who wished there was a book written for beginners. In Toni Morrison's words, "If there's a book that you want to read, but it hasn't been written yet, then you must write it." CEOs, artists, entrepreneurs, and professionals have great ideas in them that people want to know, but they seldom write a book. I believe it would be an injustice not to allow those valuable ideas to see the light of day.

It's worthwhile remembering that social media posts and blogs have a limited shelf life, but a book can be passed through several generations. So, you can wait for years and find the right time (read *never*). Or, you can turn the pages and get started right now. What is it going to be? Now? Or, never?

I encourage you to enjoy this journey.

CHAPTER 1

Why Do You Want to Write a Book?

A FRIEND OF MINE has been telling me for the last five years that he wants to write a book. Has he got down to writing it? Has he finished it? The answer is no. Being called a published author has its charms. People are smitten by the novelty and the instant credibility that comes with being a published author.

However, remember, writing is a lot of hard work. It takes at least one hundred hours of sweat, tears, and discipline to write a book. But if you're prepared to put in the time and get the job done, the rewards can be great. If you can keep doing it over and over again, you can impact a lot of people with your writing.

The reason I ask, "Why do you want to write a book?" is to get you motivated with a purpose. When things get tough, your purpose will fuel you to keep going. The trick is never to stop. Even if you write fewer words, just keep going. So, let's start with your purpose. What is your purpose in writing a book? What is it that makes you wake up early in the morning and type those words into your word processor? Are you craving sharing your stories with the world? Or maybe you're looking for an escape?

For me, writing is like meditation. It serves as an escape from the world. I also want to share my experiences with my audience. I remember a professor in college telling me, "We learn more by teaching than by being a student." Whenever I write a book on a topic, I realize that there is so much that I don't know. Today, writing has become so much a part of me that I enjoy every moment of writing, learning, and sharing. I believe all the knowledge that we have gained over the years during our lives is meant to be shared. Writing every day means that my mind is ripe with ideas, and I become more observant of what's going on around me. I'm researching all the time. A lot of the research I do entails reading, and I probably read more books now than I have ever done. That's because there's a strong link between being a good reader and becoming a good writer.

The thought of writing every day might seem intimidating at first, but you'll undoubtedly discover, as I have, that the more you keep doing it, the easier it gets—until it quickly becomes second nature.

At this stage, it may be helpful to think about some of the reasons why people want to write a book. Here's an example from my own life: A while ago, I was staying at a backpacker's hostel in Mumbai, where I got friendly with a financial services professional in his late twenties. He had traveled to several cities across India and wanted to write a book on how travelers could have a holistic experience by journeying across the country. Most travel guides talk about the same architectural wonders, which are common knowledge to most travelers. One can find these common places to visit on almost every blog post across the internet. But what if he wrote about unusual places, like the neighborhood tea stall, where eccentric people hang out, have fun conversations, and build memories?

The reason this young man wanted to write a book was because he had a story he wanted to tell. All the great memories he had experienced could be put into a book. It's a shame that many of our memories and experiences go with us to our grave. A great book lives forever. Several generations can benefit from a great book. Even if a tourist destination is destroyed, it can stay in the memories of travelers, which can be shared in a book and experienced by readers vicariously.

Some people write a book because they are rather vain and enjoy the feeling of pride that comes with being a published author. To them, being published is more of an ego boost than anything else. Nothing wrong with that! Who am I to judge? Some people think social status is as important as money and relationships.

I met a person at a recent event who had studied in the best universities in the world. He was educated, smart, had a high paying job, and some serious social swag. One of the reasons for him writing and publishing a book was to boost his social currency. We call it vanity publishing. Many publishing houses that are vanity publishers charge authors a fee to publish their books.

Traditional publishers make money from the sale of their author's books. They'll agree to publish a book if they believe it can sell. That's the reason traditional publishers reject the majority of the book proposals they receive—they don't see a market for them. However, a vanity publisher makes money by charging authors a fee. Most books published by vanity publishing houses are bought by the author to distribute at events as a promotional tool.

Families, individuals, and even companies around the world use vanity publishing to share their stories and leave a legacy for future generations.

I believe everyone should write a book because everyone has a story to tell. The most common comment I hear is, "There are so many authors out there already, and so many people have already covered the topic I have in mind. How can I add something new or write something different that hasn't been covered before?" Good question, and here's the answer: The topic you have in mind might have been covered before, but nobody has said it in your voice. It's not that nobody has written a book on how to write a non-fiction book—there are probably thousands of them—but the difference is that I've written the book in my voice. My writing style and organization of this book may not resonate with everybody, but I have an audience that loves and supports my writing by buying and sharing my work.

My first book was a Do-It-Yourself (DIY) guide. The reason I published that book was to help people write a business plan. It was only accidentally that, through this experience, I realized that writing and publishing the book went a long way towards building my credibility with readers. So, while the book wasn't exactly a bestseller, it nevertheless opened doors for me in other ways.

In the business world, the value you bring to the table is important. However, people hire you based on the perceived value you bring to the deal. It's a little like going out on a date; you might be a great guy or girl, but your perfect partner must agree to go out on a date with you before they see your value. Sometimes, we just need that one meeting with an important person to get our business or career moving. A bestselling book can increase your perceived value. It can open doors that were previously closed to you.

Trainers, coaches, and consultants often publish books to position themselves as authorities in their niche. A book is a part of their personal brand. If you write and publish a book on a certain topic, then you will quickly be perceived as an expert on that topic. Although authors like Brian Tracy, Stephen Covey, Dale Carnegie, Tony Robbins, and Robert Kiyosaki have bestsellers in their name, they generate a substantial part of their incomes from consulting, workshops, and selling online courses. For these authors, the book is a marketing tool to sell their other products.

Finally, some authors want to make money simply by selling their books. If an author makes a profit of $2 from the sale of each book, and sells 10,000 copies, that is $20,000 in profit. Not enough to replace your full-time income. However, if an author sells 100,000 copies of their book, that is $200,000 in profit. Not bad, right?

How Do We Calculate Profits for a Self-Published Author?

It's simple. Profits are calculated as your share of royalties minus printing costs. Let's say you price your book at $10. If it's a 200-page book, the cost of printing is approximately $3, your share of royalties from an online platform like Amazon is 60%; in this case, your profit is 60% of $10, which is $6 minus printing costs of $3. This equals a profit of $3. Of course, the profits will vary depending on the retailer and the distribution platform you choose. Most people writing their first non-fiction book are mainly writing the book to build their authority within their chosen field. However, some people might be looking to make a full-time income from the royalties of book sales.

Many people who have published non-fiction books in the past will tell you that it's not possible to make a full-time income from being a published author. That may well be true in most cases, but not all. There are thousands of people around the world who make a full-time income from publishing books.

What Does It Take to Earn a Full-Time Income from Self-Publishing Books?

#1 Consistent Effort

What does this mean? It means writing every single day, not just on the days you feel like it. It's highly unlikely that you'll make a full-time income from writing just one book. Most people I know who make a full-time income from book royalties write at least four books a year.

#2 Build an Audience

Your income from royalties will depend on an audience that is hungry to buy your book, likes your writing, believes in you, and is willing to buy from you every time you hit the publish button.

In the earlier paragraph, we spoke about selling 100,000 books to earn a full-time income from book royalties. Most authors don't sell more than ten copies of their books. If a first-time author is targeting 100,000 copies, imagine how many people they need to have on their mailing list.

My experience as a writer and publisher tells me that a mailing list is one of the most important pieces of the sales puzzle for an author. It's not the number of people on your mailing list that matters, but the number of raving fans. How many of them on your list are willing to buy your books? If you have a million people on your list, but none of them are willing to buy from you, then is the list really valuable? However, if you have just 1000 people on your list, and 100% of the people on your list buy your book, this list is far more valuable.

Now, hitting that magic 100,000 number in book sales. Is it possible? Read on, and I'll show you that it is possible, and how you can achieve it.

First, you don't need 100,000 people to buy your books. You can get 10,000 people to buy 10 of your books. Does that mean you should write ten books to get to 100,000? It's a lot easier making money from 10 books than it is from one. If you have just one book, once you sell that one book to your audience, you have nothing else to sell them, unless you are using the book as bait to sell online courses or subscriptions to a membership site.

Whatever your reasons for writing a book, be clear about what they are and set yourself realistic expectations. Being clear about your purpose in writing a book is going to help you keep going when things get tough. Experienced authors will tell you that you don't have to be perfect. It is true. Sometimes, all it takes is putting in the time and effort and ignoring your fears. We may fear that nobody might read our book. Our family and friends may ridicule us for writing a crappy book. But as Jeff Goins said,

> *"The book you actually write is better than the one you dream of writing."*

I want to inspire you to take action and write your first non-fiction book. I wish you all the best on this wonderful journey.

CHAPTER 2

Types of Nonfiction Books

DID YOU EVER THINK of writing a book about your foot? Or your dog, cat, or even your friendly neighbor? The beauty of publishing is that you can write a book about almost anything. There are no restrictions on the kind of books one can write. Thanks to self-publishing, anyone in the world can be a published author. It's a purely democratic process.

If you browse through Amazon's book section or walk into a bookstore, you'll see books on almost every topic. As you are probably aware, books are generally divided into two main categories—the first of which is fiction, which involves imaginary stories. It is designed to entertain readers.

Non-fiction is a whole different ball game. Stretching the truth is not acceptable in non-fiction. Making up stories in your memoir, autobiography, or even in your how-to book is not acceptable in non-fiction. Since this book is about writing your first non-fiction book, we won't go into the details of how to write a fiction book.

My guidelines will deal purely with writing non-fiction. So, let's look at some of the most popular types of non-fiction books.

Types of Nonfiction Books

Typically, most non-fiction books fall into one of four types—self-help, memoirs, autobiographies, and anthologies.

Self-Help Books

The self-help category includes books that help readers improve a specific skill or transform themselves in some way. The author typically needs to have expertise on a certain topic to write a book in this category. For example, say you decide to write a book on becoming a good photographer, then having some expertise in photography would be a big advantage.

Typically, business leaders, subject matter experts, trainers, consultants, and professionals write books in their areas of expertise, as they possess extensive knowledge or insider information of their field and want to share their expertise for the benefit of others.

Experience tells us that there is no better way to learn something than from someone who has been there and done it successfully.

Memoirs

Memoirs are the personal stories of the author. They can include events, moments in time, and specific experiences taken from the author's life that they want to share with others. Memoirs are slightly different from autobiographies.

Autobiographies generally deal with the entire lifetime of an author and include all the important events, while a memoir is usually made up of stories from a particular category or a specific period from an author's life.

Some examples of a memoir include Barack Obama's *Dreams from My Father: A Story of Race and Inheritance*, Ted Kennedy's *True Compass*, and Sidney Sheldon's *The Other Side of Me*. The great thing about a memoir is that anyone can write one—you don't have to be a famous person or a subject-matter expert. If you decide you want to go down the memoir route, there are several themes to choose from. Here are some of the most widely used memoir themes:

Inspirational Memoir

The inspiration theme takes the reader from a story of adversity to victory. The author narrates incidents from their life that have inspired them to become a better person. *The Bright Hour* by Nina Riggs is an example of an inspirational memoir, where the author writes about the experience of being diagnosed with breast cancer at the age of thirty-seven.

An inspirational memoir can be about anything that has inspired the author in her life. It doesn't need to be life-changing but can be inspirational in little ways. The inspirational memoir documents and shares the inspirational moments of the author's life.

Nostalgia Memoir

It's safe to say that we love a little nostalgia from time to time—looking back to past times and reflecting on what has changed can be enjoyable. For example, I've often noticed how cities can change drastically over a relatively short period. I live in Bangalore, a city that has dramatically changed over the years. My hometown was once a small place that had a population of fewer than one million people. Today, it's a major city with a population of over ten million people. Peoples' lifestyles have changed. Modern Bangalore sees a constant inflow and outflow of people. I could write a memoir about the old city that instills nostalgia in those readers who've lived here for many years and recall the old days with affection.

Confessional Memoir

This type of memoir is popular with readers because they often involve the author confessing their secrets to the world or trying to set the record straight and tell the world the truth about something that happened to them. James Lasdun, in his confessional memoir, shares his story about the horrifying experience of finding himself the object of the dangerous obsession of a former student with mental health problems. Alternatively, an author might decide to write about all their past lovers in a confessional memoir. For those who have dated famous people, this type of kiss-and-tell confessional memoir can often prove very successful—and lucrative.

Besides love, people have also written about addiction, divorce, and adoption, amongst other relatable topics. Lifting the lid on their secrets sometimes liberates the author. However, it's worth remembering that writing a confessional memoir can sometimes put authors in a vulnerable position, where they may become open to, for example, legal action. But a confessional memoir doesn't need to be negative but can focus instead on the positive experiences in a person's life.

Travel Memoir

Travel writing is one of the most popular niches in the online space. There are probably more travel stories on blogs and social media than any other niche in the world. Bloggers are happy to write about a place in return for free accommodation and air tickets. It's a niche that's popular and in constant demand.

If you are already a travel blogger, why not write a travel memoir documenting your travel memories? This could provide you with an additional income stream, as well as an opportunity to increase your visibility and open you up to a whole new audience.

Celebrity Memoir

In some countries, people are obsessed with celebrities. They want to know everything that's happening in the lives of their favorite stars. People from glamorous professions like modeling and acting can attain celebrity status because their work is visible to the world. It's not uncommon to see celebrities get six-figure book deals because people want to read their stories. If you're a celebrity, born to one, or married to one, then you have the ideal opportunity to write a celebrity memoir.

Political Memoir

In politics, most things are private and don't come out into the open. We see sitcoms and movies that deal with political events, but we can never be sure that we are being presented with the truth. Readers who love politics want to know the truth about what happened behind the scenes. Plus, reading the memoir of a politician is a good way to gain an understanding of the life of a politician.

Tony Blair, Barack Obama, Hilary Clinton, and David Cameron have all written memoirs. They've taken the opportunity to give their side of the story about what happened when they were in office. If you're a politician, or know a politician, you could write or co-write a memoir with them.

Sports Memoirs

The great soccer player Pele wrote a memoir, *Why Soccer Matters*. Nadia Comaneci wrote a memoir called *Letters to a Young Gymnast*. Julia Edelman's *Restless: A Memoir* made it to the New York Times Bestseller list. Usually, sportspeople write their memoirs after their playing days are over. However, that's not always the case—they can write a sports memoir during their playing days too.

Humorous Memoirs

Do you want to make people laugh with funny stories? Comedian and actress Mindy Kaling's memoir *Is Everyone Hanging Out Without Me?* showcases moments of Mindy's life and her observations on life, friendship, and Hollywood. Since Mindy is a comedy writer, you can expect to find her writing funny and humorous.

One of the things about comedy is that the more miserable you find your life, the funnier the audience will think you are. It's as if misery is funny. But a humorous memoir doesn't need to focus solely on funny stories. You could pick a serious topic and give it a humorous angle. For example, you could decide to write about a heartbreak and give it a humorous take.

I like humor, but I don't try to be funny in my books. I just speak from my heart and try to do justice to my reader by fulfilling the objective of the book.

Food Memoirs

The recent rise of the celebrity chef has made food memoirs very popular with readers. I've heard stories of people who travel the world simply to explore the many different types of cuisine on offer in other cultures. If you're a chef, a nutritionist, food historian, or simply a food enthusiast, you could write a memoir that documents your memories of food.

Relationship Memoirs

Another topic that is extremely popular on the internet is dating and relationships. The biggest problem with dating advice is that everyone thinks they are qualified to advise on it. An alternative angle could be writing a memoir on dating. It could involve all the relationships you've been in and what has worked and what hasn't worked. Doesn't it make more sense to share your experiences with readers rather than just giving plain advice on dating? Or, you could even write a book on being single, as author Kate Bolick has, in her bestseller *Spinster: Making a Life of One's Own*.

Family Memoir

Ever thought about giving a gift to your 90-year-old grandfather? A Rolls Royce might be a great gift, an expensive one, but will it make him happy? Writing a memoir about your family might make a better and cheaper gift. You could put together a collection of stories that have been passed to you from your grandfather. Wouldn't it be a great gift not just to your grandfather but also to future generations? It could make everybody in your family happy—and even become a family heirloom.

I love family memoirs because they are personal, emotional, and there is always a story that touches your heart. James McBride's *The Color of Water: A Black Man's Tribute to His White Mother* is a story about the author's mother, who married a black man before the civil rights movement in America. Another great memoir is Khizr Khan's *An American Family: A Memoir of Hope and Sacrifice*. It's the story of an immigrant from Pakistan who grew up in America. As you can see, family memoirs come in all shapes and forms.

Business and Work Memoir

If you are an entrepreneur or work in the corporate world, people who want to get into similar professions will probably want to read about your experiences. *My Father's Business: The Small-Town Values That Built Dollar General into a Billion-Dollar Company* by Cal Turner, Jr. and Rob Simbeck is a memoir about the values that built the Dollar General company into a billion-dollar business. It's a retail chain that operates 15,000 stores across America and is listed on the New York stock exchange.

Another work memoir, *Nickel and Dimed: On (Not) Getting by in America* by Barbara Ehrenreich, is a story of American workers who work on minimum wage. The author talks about how it's not possible to survive with one job in America, and a minimum wage worker may need two or more jobs to survive.

If you dig deep and brainstorm, you might find that you will come up with several stories to include in your work memoir. Many of these stories might seem obvious and routine to you but may not be evident to other people outside your profession. I remember talking to a doctor about my publishing business—many of the things obvious to me seemed like rocket science to him. Our trade might be routine and obvious to us but not to someone who is not in our profession.

Fitness Memoirs

I have always worked hard at staying fit, but I understand that this is a challenge for many people. Being overweight or skinny are emotional issues for people, and many have been hurt by being body-shamed publicly. Writing a memoir about their fitness journey could liberate the author from a lot of negative emotions and might also inspire other people who are traveling the same path.

Parenting Memoirs

If you've been a parent and raised a child, you know how challenging it can be. Writing about it can be an inspiration to everyone who has experienced or is about to experience the unique joys and pitfalls of parenthood.

Laura June's *Now My Heart is Full* is a story about how having a child of our own can change the way we perceive our mothers. It's a great story of motherhood. If you're a parent, then writing a memoir on parenthood can be an educational tale for anyone who is looking to be a parent.

Anthologies

If you don't have the time to write a complete book, then anthologies present the opportunity to create a book by bringing several authors together. In an anthology, several authors come together, and each contributes a chapter in the book. For example, if you can get twenty authors to contribute one chapter each, then you'll soon have enough content for an entire book.

Now that we've reached the end of the chapter, have you identified the non-fiction book you want to write? Or, have all the possibilities covered here left you feeling a bit confused? Don't worry if you're still on the fence—the important thing is to keep reading. You'll eventually find your way.

CHAPTER 3

The Most Important Quality for Writing Success

THE GREEK PHILOSOPHER ARISTOTLE said:

"We are what we repeatedly do. Excellence, then, is not an act. It's a habit."

A writer on the internet claims it wasn't Aristotle's quote, but it was Will Durant who first said it in his book *The Story of Philosophy*.[1] It doesn't matter who said it first, what's important is to take note and understand that developing good habits is critical to achieving success as an author.

I'm told that every second person wants to write a book, but so few of them actually do it. Meanwhile, their competition is churning out a new book every three months. But how is that even possible? It makes one wonder if there is a secret formula or recipe for successfully writing and publishing a book that only those prolific writers have discovered.

When I was younger, I played a lot of tennis. Despite waking up early in the morning not being one of my favorite activities, I still did it because I loved the sport. As I grew older and began attending college, I stopped playing tennis.

My college days were filled with late-night parties and hanging out with friends until the wee hours of the morning. That meant I got into the habit of waking up late, something that carried over into other areas of life. For instance, once I started a business, I would begin my workday towards noon and end the day late. For me, waking up early and getting up was one of the most difficult tasks of my life.

In the meantime, I also started writing. Many authors have said that they found early morning to be the best time of the day to write. However, in my case, I wrote late into the night because I didn't have to worry about waking up early.

But writing late at night didn't seem sustainable. I knew that I wanted to develop a way of writing that would work for the long-term. That's when I started researching the habits of successful authors whom I wanted to emulate. I wanted to be like them and be able to write all the stories locked up in my mind. I came across authors who had written over a hundred books. I wondered if I could do the same.

If I wanted to produce that many books, then I would have to work hard at cultivating lifelong writing habits. It dawned on me that motivation would not be enough.

Neeraj Agnihotri, author of *Procrasdemon: The Artist's Guide To Liberation From Procrastination,* said, "Habits stay with you even when you don't have the motivation."[2]

Writing a book from start to finish can take several months, sometimes years. There are going to be days when you're bored and won't feel like writing. You might just stare at the blank page, without a single word coming to mind. Well, no matter if the words only come with difficulty—you've still got to keep going. It's at this point that you'll see why I say that it's essential to develop good writing habits. Because good writing habits will keep you forging ahead when inspiration or energy is lacking.

We spend a lot of our lives on autopilot. We follow the same routines every day: We wake up, brush our teeth, have breakfast, and head to work without even thinking. Our daily behaviors are so deeply ingrained in us that it is difficult to change. So, when we set ourselves a new goal, we may need to abandon old habits and cultivate new ones. Vince Lombardi said, "Winning is not a sometime thing; it's an all-the-time thing. You don't win once in a while, you don't do things right once in a while, you do them right all the time. Winning is a habit."[3]

Habits are daily actions, routines, rituals, and behaviors that we do almost automatically without even thinking about them, or perhaps even noticing them.

The human brain is the organ that controls all our functions, from breathing to walking. The basal ganglia, the part of our brain that is located near the forebrain and the top of the midbrain, controls habits, routine behaviors, and procedural learning. It acts somewhat like a computer: Once an action becomes a habit, the part of our brain that stores the habit function goes to sleep; the brain records the action associated with the habit and doesn't need to do any further work except keep repeating it automatically when needed.

The human brain has developed an intelligent system where habits are stored and repeated in order to reduce the effort that we spend on routine activities. Day to day things, like brushing our teeth, become so automatic that we don't even have to think where we should put the toothpaste on the brush.

Habits are the brain's system that helps us become productive by automating routine tasks so that we can focus on things that require attention.

While some habits are developed consciously, others are developed unconsciously.

For example, smokers often say they picked up the habit of smoking when they spent time with friends, a parent, or the popular guy in college who smoked. Then, later in life, when they want to kick the smoking habit, they find it difficult because the habit is firmly ingrained in their system. Over the years, we pick up habits from friends, family, society, and popular culture that we're not even aware of.

It's easy to see that an action that is repeated often can become a habit. As authors, if we develop good habits, finishing that book is going to be almost automatic.

> Seth Godin has been writing every single day for the last eleven years. He says, "Streaks require commitment at first, but then the commitment turns into a practice, and the practice into a habit. Habits are much easier to maintain than commitments."[4]

The first writing goal I set myself was to write every single day. I don't worry about the number of words I write, instead I just stick to writing for at least one hour every day. I chose one hour per day because I think that it is achievable for most people. There's usually room in our busy lives to commit to one hour a day of writing, even if we have a family and a full-time job to manage.

"I write every morning," said Ernest Hemingway.

When I researched the writing process of some of the world's most successful authors, I found that they had a consistent schedule throughout their lives.

> Hemingway further went on to add, "When I am working on a book or a story, I write every morning as soon after first light as possible. There is no one to disturb you and it is cool or cold, and you come to your work and warm as you write."[5]

Barbara Kingsolver, author of several New York Times Bestsellers, says, "I tend to wake up very early. Too early. Four o'clock is standard. My morning begins with trying not to get up before the sun rises. But when I do, it's because my head is too full of words, and I just need to get to my desk and start dumping them into a file. I always wake with sentences pouring into my head. So, getting to my desk every day feels like a long emergency. It's a funny thing: People often ask how I discipline myself to write. I can't begin to understand the question. For me, the discipline is turning off the computer and leaving my desk to do something else."[6]

Unlike Barbara, I'm not naturally an early bird. After years of writing, I've settled down to a routine of writing after 6 am, which, for me, is the most productive part of my day. If I do occasionally find myself writing at 4 am on some days, like some of the bestselling authors, it's usually because I haven't slept the entire night. However, I'm learning to wake up early, but it's a constant battle that I am trying hard to win. On those days when I have woken up early, I've surprised myself by writing more words than I've ever written.

We have the highest amount of energy as soon as we wake up. It's perhaps the best time to write, even for night owls like me. So, writing that book and finishing it might mean having to sacrifice TV time or an activity that is not adding value to your life. Try sitting down and making a list of your daily activities. You'll probably find an activity or two that isn't adding any value to your life. Once you've identified them, you can eliminate those activities and invest that time in writing your book.

I found that, like a lot of people today, I was wasting too much time on social media. So, I decided to take the unprecedented step of unfollowing every single person on all my social media profiles. I can personally vouch for the fact that life has been so much better since then. I no longer waste time on unnecessary discussions and arguments on social media. To make things even easier and more time-saving, I also automate all my work-related social media activities, which has saved me an enormous amount of time. That's why I'm sure that each of you can also find an activity in your schedules that can be eliminated, which can buy you that crucial one hour to write your book.

If waking up an hour early and writing your book isn't a realistic option for you, maybe you can cut short your lunch or tea break at work? If you want to finish writing that book, the first habit to develop is to write every single day, whether you feel like it or not.

> Internationally acclaimed author Khaled Hosseini says, "I have met so many people who say they've got a book in them, but they've never written a word. To be a writer—this may seem trite, I realize—you have to actually write. You have to write every day, and you have to write whether you feel like it or not."[7]

I advise that you start writing at the exact same time every day. To help you with this, try to remove any obstacles to your writing. I write as soon as I wake up, before I even shower or brush my teeth. I like to get my writing out of the way before my workday begins. Conditions may not always be perfect for writing, but you've got to experiment and then settle for something that works for you.

Find a comfortable spot, either at a café or in your home, and sit in that same spot every day. The decision on when, where, and for how long you write should be made upfront.

Start small: Don't be too hard on yourself if something causes you to miss your schedule. The trick is just to keep trying until you succeed. Any new habit is hard to develop, but, with persistence, you'll find that you'll get there sooner than you think.

I always find I get too many ideas! For instance, at any one time, there are several books I want to write. I don't want to stop at one. The challenge for me is to put aside my ideas and work on just one idea. If this is you and you have several book ideas all at the same time, don't let them slip away, but save them on a spreadsheet. That way, you can safely forget about them while you write the current book and come back to them later when you're ready to write another. But, for the time being, put all your focus into the one book you are writing right now.

Writers are all different: I know people who've completed writing a book in a few months, and others who have taken two years to complete theirs. What's the common trait these two groups of people share? Both of them finished writing their book.

Most authors want to write a book and get it published, but to do that, you must first finish writing it. It's nice to aim for perfection, but usually, 'good enough' is fine. Finish writing your book. Then, the next job is to find a good editor to polish your manuscript.

When I started my life as an entrepreneur back in 2004, I made the mistake of trying to do too many things at the same time. The problem with that was I couldn't complete most of the things I started. We only have 24 hours in a day, and we don't have the time to do everything we desire. We've got to say no to a lot of things. So, I made a resolution to finish every project that I start. When it comes to writing your book, you should try to do the same and be committed to finishing what you start.

Finally, measure your work. I find that maintaining a spreadsheet where I log in the number of hours I spend on writing and the number of words I write each day is immensely helpful in checking my progress. At the end of the month, I can measure the number of days, hours, and words I wrote that month. By measuring my work, I know if I am becoming more productive or not.

At the beginning of this chapter, I noted that one out of two people want to write a book, but few of them succeed. There's no doubt that writing a book and getting it published is likely to be one of the most challenging tasks that you undertake in life. Even professional writers will tell you that it's a struggle. However, by cultivating good habits, writing a book can become much easier. The trick, as those successful writers have said, is to keep writing and try to get a little better every day. Yes, there will be obstacles along the way, as well as days when you look at the blank page and simply feel that the ideas and the words have dried up, and you'd much rather be doing something else. But don't give up—just keep going. Don't stop. If you stick to the methods discussed in this chapter, you could soon find yourself producing several books throughout your lifetime.

Notes

[1] Caelan Huntress, "My Favorite Quote of All Time Is a Misattribution.," Medium (Mission.org, August 25, 2017), https://medium.com/the-mission/my-favourite-quote-of-all-time-is-a-misattribution-66356f22843d.

[2] Neeraj Agnihotri, *Procrasdemon: The Artist's Guide To Liberation From Procrastination*, accessed June 1, 2020, https://www.amazon.com/Procrasdemon-Artists-Guide-LIberation-Procrastination-ebook/dp/B07SG5VGGY/.

[3] Vincent T Lombardi, "What It Takes to Be Number One," What It Takes to be Number One | Vince Lombardi, accessed June 1, 2020, http://www.vincelombardi.com/number-one.html.

[4] Seth Godin, "Streaks," Seth's Blog, August 7, 2019, https://seths.blog/2019/08/streaks/.

[5] Mason Currey, *Daily Rituals: How Great Minds Make Time, Find Inspiration, and Get to Work* (Picador; Main Market Ed. edition, 2014).

[6] Michael Breus, *The Power of When: Learn the Best Time to Do Everything* (London, UK: Vermilion, 2016).

[7] Debra Stuart, "Khaled Hosseini," Khaled Hosseini | The Story Mint, 2012, https://www.thestorymint.com/content/khaled-hosseini.

CHAPTER 4

How to Come up with a Book Title?

HOW IMPORTANT IS THE title of a book? Why do authors fret over a book title? I'm currently in despair about coming up with a fitting title for my book. I've already shortlisted a few titles and have done a beta test with my audience, but I still seem to be a long way away from thinking up something catchy.

How many times have you heard the phrase, "Don't judge a book by its cover?" And yet, that's quite literally, what we do when we buy a book. And what's on the cover? The book title.

Readers will most likely see the title of the book before they even see the cover because the title shows up in search results on Google, Amazon, and other online retailers.

Ideally, a title should describe your entire content in one word. A reader should understand what the book is about and why they should read it. When you consider that non-fiction books are solving a problem for the reader, hitting the pain point in the title can give the author an edge over a random title that fails to encapsulate what the book offers.

The title needs to not only resonate with your audience but should also be easy to discover for readers who are searching online. The search factor plays a crucial role when you're crafting a book title.

When you're self-publishing a book, there's no publisher to suggest a marketable title for you—a self-published author is her own publisher. So, it's your job to come up with a title that is marketable and sets up the right expectations for the reader. Even if you do have a publisher, it's good to take control and come up with a title that sells your book.

As a rookie blogger, I noticed that most of my gurus suggested spending as much time writing the headline as writing the entire article. A book is no different. The fortunes of several books have improved significantly after being taken off the shelf and republished with a different title and cover.

The overriding purpose of your book title is to catch the attention of your audience—notice the emphasis on YOUR: You must know your target audience. I recommend researching other books in your genre to see what kind of titles your audiences are attracted to.

I am not a big fan of book titles that don't give my audience clues as to what the book is about. I want the purpose of my book to be clear and explicit, which doesn't necessarily mean that "out-of-the-box" book titles don't work; if you feel you must have such a title, then you can always add a subtitle that gives a more elaborate description of your book.

Take a look at some of these book titles: *Creative Confidence, How to Win Friends and Influence People, Talking to Strangers: What We Should Know about the People We Don't Know*. In all these cases, the title clearly states the purpose of the book, so the reader knows what to expect.

One of my earliest books was called *How to Write a Business Plan for Astonishing Results in Just 3 Days*. The purpose of the book was to give people a step-by-step process for writing a business plan in three days or less.

Although the title is slightly lengthy, my audience immediately understood the purpose of the book just by reading its title.

Before you write a book title, it's always helpful to know the genre, the objective of the book, your audience, as well as your innermost reasons for writing it. For instance, I like adding a bit of emotion to the title—as human beings, we are emotional creatures, and a little emotion can pique the reader towards your book.

Besides being attention-grabbing and giving information to the reader, a book title should ideally be easy to remember, memorable, create curiosity, and it should not be too long. Short titles work better because they fit into most conversations, both online and offline. Remember, people, including us, hear about books from family, friends, peers, and social media, so it's vital that they are easy to share.

If you can come up with a snappy, one-word title that has all the attributes explained above, there's nothing so effective. Plus, you can add a further description in the sub-title. Take Sarah Marsh's book *Heartland*, for example: The title hints at a political book rather than a memoir, yet the subtitle, *A Memoir of Working Hard and Being Broke in the Richest Country on Earth,* gives a much clearer description of the content of the book.

A subtitle is a useful way to add a bit more information about the book for the reader. It's a big opportunity to grab the reader's attention, which is especially important if your main title is a single word or out-of-the-box.

Tim Ferris' book title *4-hour Workweek* creates a little curiosity that intrigues readers. When I first saw the title, I instantly thought it was a book about productivity, where the reader learns to manage a 40-hour workweek in four hours. But the subtitle, *Escape the*

9-5, Live Anywhere and Join the New Rich, explains the title a bit further. By reading the subtitle, I realize the book is not just about productivity; it's also about getting rich and escaping the 9-to-5 grind.

The *4-hour Workweek* is a perfect example of how to successfully create curiosity with an intriguing title, then adding a description of the book in the subtitle.

Another book title I like is Seth Godin's *The Dip.* Initially, when I read the title, it made me curious as to what the book was about, which drew me in. Then, I read the subtitle— *A Little Book That Teaches You When To Quit (And When To Stick).* The purpose is crystal clear in the subtitle—it's a book that teaches the reader when to quit and when to stick.

When I wrote my first book, I didn't think hard enough about the title, because I didn't realize the value of a good title. I've found that, when I speak at conferences and seminars, a long title can sometimes be hard to share. So, I've made peace with myself and now try to keep my titles as short as possible. This takes some discipline on my part because, as you can tell, I naturally tend to like long titles.

Another important aspect of titles is their relation to keywords. SEO (Search Engine Optimization) is more important today than ever before, with millions of us discovering stuff through searching on Google.

The way search engines work means that strategically placing a keyword in the title or subtitle can make your book show up on search results, thereby bringing in new readers. As you can see, developing an understanding of the importance of selecting the right book title can be crucial to success.

Now, let's break down what we've learned into a step-by-step process.

Step 1: Book Genre

The first thing to do is to write down the genre of your book, its purpose (what it will do for the reader), and your ideal target audience.

I consider most non-fiction books to fall into the self-help category because they are helping people become better at something. By understanding the genre of your book, you can find out what kind of titles your audience is used to. This will require doing a little research.

Then, write down the objective or purpose of your book. I've found that the best way to figure out your objective is to ask yourself the question: Why should my target audience read my book? For instance, the objective of this book is to *help people write their first non-fiction book*. Your title must reflect your objective.

When I first started in business, I often met people who constantly claimed that their target market is "everybody." Unfortunately, that doesn't work, because it's too unspecific: Identifying your target audience means that you can focus your energy on writing specifically to meet the needs of that audience.

For example, your target audience could be teenagers in high school, or entrepreneurs, self-employed professionals, doctors, engineers, or your immediate local community. Identify who it is and write it down, because the clearer you are about your target audience, the easier it will be to come up with a title that resonates with those readers.

Step 2: Identify a Keyword

Finding a keyword involves using a keyword research tool. Google has a free keyword research tool called Keyword Planner.

Here are some basics to help get you started: First go to Google Keyword Planner—it's a free keyword tool that helps you to find low-competition, high-volume keywords. You can find this useful tool by searching for "Google Keyword Planner" on Google.com. Once you've found the tool, log in with your Google account and click on "discover keywords." A search box will pop up, showing already discovered keywords. Then, enter a word or phrase related to your book, and the tool will produce a list of keywords, along with the number of average monthly searches and competition related to it. You can then choose one or two relevant keywords with high-volume and low competition, which are going to lay the foundation for your book title.

Step 3: Research Popular Book Titles in Your Genre

Once you've identified a keyword, the next step is to search for bestselling books in your genre to see what kind of book titles your target audience is buying. I don't suggest copying titles of bestsellers, but it's well worth just browsing through the most successful to get a better idea of what you're aiming for.

Amazon is the best place to find bestsellers in your genre. Go to Amazon's website, click on your book category, and check out a selection of the most popular books in your genre. This research will give you a good starting point for coming up with a great book title.

Step 4: Brainstorm

Once you've got a few ideas about book titles that work and what they look like, the next step is to come up with a list of your own.

I suggest writing down everything that comes to mind, even if it doesn't seem to make much sense at first. Once you come up with a list of, say, 100 possible book titles, then pick the five strongest. While the majority of the titles may seem like gibberish, sheer quantity means that there is always quality hidden somewhere in there. Remember, you only need one great title for your book.

Another possibility is to use online tools specifically designed to help you generate book titles. Here's a selection of popular online tools that enable you to enter a keyword and have the software generate titles for you.

https://www.portent.com/tools/title-maker
https://www.adazing.com/book-title-generator/
https://kopywritingkourse.com/book-title-generator/

Step 5: Make a Shortlist

Many authors believe that the audience is the decision-maker when it comes to the title and content of a book. But, in reality, it's your book, so if you aren't excited about your title, then it's unlikely that potential readers will be! So, before you take your title to a beta audience, pick the title that most excites you.

Of course, there's no doubt that market research is important, but it can only take you so far. A book is not always about giving an audience what they want, it's about introducing them to something they never knew existed before.

Step 6: Do a Poll to See How the Title Resonates with Your Audience

This is where we put our friends to work: Pick someone who you think best represents your target audience, then send them your shortlisted titles, along with a message asking which of the books they are most likely to buy.

Another way to gauge responses to your title is to try doing the same poll online on social media and with your newsletter subscribers using a survey site like "Survey Monkey," which allows you to collect responses through a web form.

Now, a look to the future: As you keep writing more books, you'll realize the value of your mailing list. Good authors have a mailing list of loyal readers who are not just willing to buy their books, but also provide valuable feedback.

Personally, I like to title my book before I start writing, but I have to admit, it doesn't always happen that way. Sometimes a good title just pops up in my head out of nowhere, and I get excited about it. Hopefully, this chapter has shown you how crafting a title for a book is one of the many challenges that authors face—but it can also be an enjoyable process.

CHAPTER 5

The Book Plan

I LIKE TO PLAN my work before I start. Planning gives me order, structure, and direction. When I was younger, I made a conscious decision to become organized and do things in an orderly manner. As Napoleon Hill said, "Plan your work and work your plan."

Imagine, you want to construct a house. How would you go about it? The logical place to start would be to meet with an architect, get them to prepare a blueprint, and then find a construction manager to implement the architect's plan.

If you started constructing a house without a plan, can you imagine what would happen? You'd be building and breaking walls based on trial and error, the project would take a lot longer than expected, and you'd probably end up spending more money than someone with a plan. Even worse, the house may never even get constructed.

The purpose of a plan is to get the desired result with the least effort, optimum productivity (more is less time), and with the least amount of stress.

Writing a book is an enormous project, but a book plan breaks down the book writing process into smaller and more manageable parts.

So, what exactly do we mean when we talk about a plan? According to the Merriam-Webster dictionary, "A plan is a detailed formulation of a program of action." I prefer a simpler definition—a plan is a set of activities designed to achieve the desired goal.

If you're reading this book, I presume that your goal is to write a non-fiction book. Keeping this goal in mind, what are the decisions that you will need to make before setting out? Here are the main ones you will need to consider:

1. The title of the book
2. Your reasons for writing the book.
3. The objective of the book
4. Your target audience
5. Why should your target audience read the book?
6. Length of the book
7. Number of chapters
8. Length of each chapter
9. List of chapters
10. Outline for each chapter

Let's go over each of these decisions one by one:

Title of the Book

If you don't have a title yet, start with a tentative title, you can always change it later. Once you've read the chapter and come up with a book title, write it down either on a sheet of paper or on your word processor.

Your Purpose for Writing the Book (Why?)

Ask yourself these questions: Why am I writing this book? What's my motivation? How is it going to change my life? Try to keep your purpose focused. There's a chapter titled "Why do you want to write a book?" Please read that chapter and write down your motivation for writing a book.

Your Target Audience

I like to think of a target audience as a homogenous group of people who are likely to buy and read my book. If you had to find a common thread among your readers and classify them as a category, what similar characteristics do you think they would have? There are two alternatives: You can either find an audience and then write a book for them. Or, you can write a book and then find an audience. In my experience, it's more effective to find an audience and write a book that is tailormade for them than the other way around.

Let's take this book, *How to Write Your First Non-Fiction Book,* for example. I decided to write the book and then find an audience. Yes, it's against what I preach. But at the time, I was so motivated to write this book that I chose to break my own rules.

I asked myself who would be interested in reading my book. The answer was anyone interested in writing a non-fiction book. But who is this anyone? Is there a way to define them? Would college students be interested in reading my book? In my opinion, it's unlikely.

How about entrepreneurs? Maybe. How about self-employed professionals like architects, doctors, dentists, corporate trainers, and consultants? Yes, they're more likely to read my book because they may want to write a book on their field of work and position themselves as an authority in their niche. Who else might be interested?

At social gatherings and conferences, I come across heads of departments, vice-presidents, and senior-level managers who are interested in writing a book. Someone with, say, more than ten years' experience in their profession might want to write a book.

Initially, I said to myself that anyone interested in writing a book is my target audience—quite a vague description. But after defining the identity of my potential readers further, I've arrived at a more descriptive target audience—entrepreneurs, self-employed professionals, and heads of departments who are over 35 years of age. Dig deeper and try to find specific characteristics that define your audience. I've found through experience that coming up with only a vague definition of 'anyone' who wants to buy my book rarely works.

Reader's Problem

Once you've identified a target audience, ask yourself, what problem does the reader have that the book is trying to solve? In my case, this book gives the reader a process to write a non-fiction book. A complete novice who has never written a book in their life should be able to write their first non-fiction book after reading this book.

Length of Your Book

I measure the length of a book by the number of words rather than the number of pages because the number of pages can vary depending on the dimensions and the design of the interior pages of the book. So, the number of words is a better measure when considering the length of a book.

If you walk into the non-fiction section of a bookstore, you'll see books of various sizes. Some will be over 300 pages, a few will be less than 150 pages, but most will be in-between that range. If you're getting published through a traditional publishing house, then your publisher may give you a word count target. If you are self-publishing, then you're the boss—you can choose the length of your book.

However, there are a few considerations you should keep in mind when choosing your ideal word count target. The most important factor is the expectation of the reader. I once wrote a book that was less than 20 pages. My mindset was to give my readers a process that would take them from point A to point B in the fastest amount of time. I got negative feedback because my readers wanted more detailed information, and they expected the book to be of a certain length.

A Hollywood movie is usually around ninety minutes in length, so moviegoers and cinemas have come to accept this as the norm. People still make movies that are longer or shorter, but filmmakers might have a hard time selling them. However, in publishing, it's not always that cut and dried. In the fiction category, some associations list the ideal size for a novel, but I'm not aware of anything like that for the non-fiction category.

The best way to figure out if your book meets reader's expectations is to check out the size of some of the bestselling books in your genre, which should give you a fair idea. The trick is to find an ideal length the reader is already used to reading.

I know my answers are not definitive, and you may have to do some research to find the ideal book length. I have identified book lengths that work for me. Of course, you can choose to follow my formula or do your own research.

The word count that works for me:

60,000 words = Ideal

60,001 words to 90,000 Words = Acceptable

30,000 words to 59,999 words = Acceptable

Below 30,000 words = Too short

Above 90,000 words = Might be too long (Consider splitting up the book into more focused topics)

This book was originally titled *How to Write, Publish, and Sell Your First Non-Fiction Book*. However, after I started writing the book, I thought to myself that there might be readers who are only beginning to write a book and may not be interested in publishing and marketing at this point. There may be others who have finished writing and publishing and are only looking for marketing help. It made more sense to split it up into three books—writing, publishing, and marketing so that readers can buy all three books together or separately, depending on their needs.

List of Chapters

A non-fiction book provides a solution to a reader's problem. It takes the reader from point A to point B. For example, Stephen Covey's *7 Habits of Highly Effective People* helps readers become more effective in life and work. Seth Godin's *The Dip* teaches people when to quit and when to stick to something.

Chapters act as a step-by-step process to take the reader from point A to point B. The easiest way to make a list of chapters is to write down the objective of the book and then make a list of steps to achieve that objective. Each step can be a chapter. For example, if the objective of your book is to teach people how to run a marathon, chapter 1 could be preparation, chapter 2 could be nutrition, chapter 3 could be running technique, and so on.

Another way is to give the reader several options to choose from rather than a list of steps. For example, one could write a book called *10 Ways to Skin a Cat*, where each chapter gives the reader one method to skin a cat.

I like to have one idea or message per chapter. I've found that if you include more than one idea per chapter, the reader is likely to lose focus. As writers, even we lose focus and drift away when we try to put too many ideas into one chapter. If you have more than one idea, consider breaking it up into more chapters.

Another decision to make is the number of chapters. There's no right answer here, but here's a method I use: I decide the length of my book in words, then I break it down into perhaps 20 or 30 chapters. For example, if I choose to write a book of 60,000 words, then I break it down into 20 chapters of 3000 words each.

You may ask, "Should every chapter be of similar length?" Let's investigate this by analyzing some bestsellers: Jack Welch's book *Winning* has 20 chapters. The longest is 28 pages, the shortest is eight pages, and there are several between eight and 28 pages. There is no uniformity in the length of each chapter.

Brian Tracy's *Hire and Keep the Best People* has 21 chapters. The longest chapter is eight pages, and the shortest is four pages. Some chapters are six pages long. The difference in pages is not as extreme as those in Jack Welch's *Winning*. The author has tried to maintain some form of uniformity in chapter length.

Authors who propagate uniformity in chapter length claim that it adds rhythm to their book, and readers know roughly the amount of time they'll spend on each chapter. Although I target a specific word count per chapter, I'm not adamant about uniformity. A target gives me the motivation to strive for something. It helps me as a writer. That's my only reason to have a target word count per chapter. If I think that a particular chapter has more information than my target word count, I continue writing until I feel the chapter is complete.

There are no rules when it comes to the number of chapters in your book or word count per chapter. If you're a self-published author, you're the boss, and you decide the chapter length. Having said that, I'd like to add that I am not a big fan of short chapters. I like my chapter length to be at least 2000 words.

Once you decide on the number of chapters and the word count, it's time to make a list of chapters.

Initially, write whatever comes to your mind. At this stage, there's no need to worry about whether they're the ones you'll finally end up with, so don't be too judgmental.

Dump every thought in your mind on a piece of paper or a word processor. Then, clean up your chapter list to include only those you want to keep. Don't worry about getting it perfectly right. Most chapter lists are imperfect at this stage. You can always come back and change it later.

I consider planning to be one of the most essential stages of writing a book. It gives the author focus. But my initial book plan is not cast in stone—I'm always willing to come back and change it if required. As you keep writing, new ideas may come up, and you can refine your plan to make it better.

CHAPTER 6

Plagiarism and Copyrights

IN 2006, KAAVYA VISHWANATH, who had just graduated from high school at the time, reportedly got a $500,000 two-book deal from a publishing company. Vishwanath gave interviews in magazines, newspapers, and on television prior to the launch of her much-publicized book How Opal Mehta Got Kissed, Got Wild, and Got a Life. The book soon made it to the New York Times bestseller list. DreamWorks even bought the movie rights to the book.

For a while, Vishwanath was touted as one of the top upcoming young novelists in America. However, Vishwanath's fame didn't last long. By April 2006, readers and media publications were calling out Vishwanath for plagiarism. Reports claimed that she had plagiarized work from several bestselling authors, namely Sophie Kinsella, Salman Rushdie, Meg Cabot, and, most notably, Megan McCafferty.

The author eventually apologized and went on to say that any similarity between her work and that of Megan McCafferty was 'unintentional and unconscious.' Her publisher recalled the novel and offered a refund to purchasers, and canceled Vishwanath's second book deal. The movie deal was also canceled. Here was a young novelist who could've had a great career as an author, but, unfortunately, allowed plagiarism to ruin it.

Let's take a closer look at the subject of plagiarism.

What Is Plagiarism?

Plagiarism is when an author claims someone else's work as their own or gives the impression that it is and fails to give credit to the original creator. For instance, if you quote someone else's words in your book, then you must mention that those are another person's words and not yours.

There are several ways of crediting an author for a sentence or paragraph of theirs that you have quoted. For example, if I want to mention Mark Twain's quote in my book, I'd say: Mark Twain said, "A person who won't read has no advantage over one who can't read." If I just said, *I believe a person who won't read has no advantage over one who can't read*, it would be plagiarism because I am claiming Mark Twain's quote as my own.

There are so many instances where authors mention sentences and paragraphs in their book without citing a source and have fallen foul of the plagiarism rule. Journalists have lost their jobs because they knocked off just one paragraph from someone else's work and forgot to cite that person.

The chances of getting caught for plagiarism are much higher today than ever before because several softwares can easily identify plagiarized parts. It's no good claiming ignorance—accidental plagiarism is as big a crime as intentional plagiarism. The punishment for plagiarism varies in different countries. In some countries, the penalty could be jail, while in others you could land a hefty fine, and be forced to give a public apology or both. The root of the word plagiarism is from the Latin phrase *plagiarius*, *which means kidnapper*.[1]

Plagiarism causes more than financial harm; it also negatively affects an author's reputation. It is difficult to rebuild the reader's trust after breaking it in such a way. I remember attending a training workshop. The trainer had copied content in his workbook from a famous author. One attendee figured it out, and the word spread. The trainer lost his reputation, and I doubt if he's recovered from that loss yet. Sometimes, the biggest losses in life are not monetary but a loss of reputation. As Warren Buffett said, "We can lose a lot of money but not our reputation."

It is common today for people to copy and paste content to their social media channels without giving credit to the original author. This may be something people get away with on social media, but if you plan on being an author, then you've got to watch out for the plagiarism trap.

Types of Plagiarism

Plagiarism comes in several different forms, which I've outlined below to make things clearer.

The most obvious is direct plagiarism, where one author copies the exact words of another author. It's a blatant copy and paste of another author's work without giving attribution to the author. If you copy and paste another author's work, you must give attribution to that author.

I remember meeting a social media marketer at a conference when I was the Managing Editor of a print magazine. He offered to write a guest column in our magazine. Since he had good knowledge of social media, I agreed to let him write for us. When he handed over the article to us, we ran a plagiarism check only to find that the majority of his article was a copy and paste from the internet. There were no citations. Although the author was a respected person in the field of social media marketing, he had no idea that he was plagiarizing content. We had to then explain to him about plagiarism and its severe consequences.

Another form of plagiarism is 'mosaic' plagiarism, where the author copies the structure or phrases of another writer and rewrites them using synonyms to disguise the fact. Although the words are different, the general meaning is the same. If the author doesn't cite the source and rewrites the content and passes it off as her own, it is still plagiarism. This kind of plagiarism is also called 'patchwork' because the author is patching phrases and words from other people's work.

Finally, there is accidental plagiarism, where the author forgets to cite the source or does not know how to cite others' work properly. The commonly used styles of citing sources are AP (Associated Press), APA (American Psychological Association), MLA (Modern Language Association), and the Chicago (Chicago Manual of Style) style. It's vital that, when you're writing your book, you choose one of these styles and stick to it throughout your book to maintain consistency. Don't change styling methods within your book, or you could confuse readers. If you choose to use the Chicago style, for example, use it throughout the book. It's sloppy to use Chicago style on one page, AP on another, and so on. Be consistent and stick to one style.

Your choice of citation style is a matter of preference rather than convention. If you are self-publishing a book, then the citation style is entirely your call. However, if you are going the traditional publishing route, then the citation style depends on your publisher.

How to Avoid Plagiarism?

All of us are influenced by certain authors and books. It's easy to paraphrase and even quote authors without even realizing that we're doing it. There's a fine line between paraphrasing and expressing your own views, and it's essential to learn the difference. Paraphrasing is rewriting someone else's sentences in your own words without changing its meaning. This is dangerous territory for writers—it can be seen as the dark borders of plagiarism. If you decide to write about someone's original idea or concept, it's safer to mention that it belongs to them, and you're only borrowing it to illustrate a point.

However, as authors, it's best to come up with our own original ideas. For that, we need to be good observers. I like to observe, analyze, and draw inferences from my observations. That allows me to be creative and come up with original ideas, and I encourage you to do the same. If you must use someone else's sentences, then make sure to cite the original author.

I strongly suggest that you come up with your own stories and develop your own voice as an author. For instance, I like to write about my personal experiences. This doesn't just help me avoid plagiarism, it also makes my content more personable. It helps my readers connect with me more intimately. I talk about my experiences, challenges, and how I overcame them. Our experiences are unique to us. Through them, our readers can vicariously experience our journey.

Now that you understand the importance of avoiding plagiarism, I strongly suggest that you consider evaluating your work by running it through some plagiarism software. There are several different packages available out there, some of them are not too expensive. The most popular plagiarism software used today is Copyscape. It's a paid option, but it's not too expensive. You simply upload your content onto Copyscape, and it will compare your content with information from all over the internet to see if there is any similar content. Another option is using the plagiarism check option on another popular software—Grammarly. It's a little bit more elaborate than Copyscape and is also a paid option. The investment in either of these softwares is not very high. I believe that, for authors, it's worth the investment because it helps us avoid any accidental plagiarism.

Copyrights

A friend of mine who is an image consultant had a misconception that if her work was not registered with the government copyright agency, then it was not protected by copyright law and anyone could copy her work without consequences. However, this is far from the truth.

Copyright law is there to prohibit anyone from copying and distributing your work without your permission, even if you don't register your content with the government's copyright office. In fact, in most countries, your content is automatically copyrighted the moment you create it. So, if someone copies your work without giving you proper credit, you can sue that person. However, the onus is on you to prove that the work belongs to you.

A copyright grants exclusive rights to the author to copy and distribute their work for a limited period. It also prohibits people from copying and distributing the work of the author without permission from the copyright holder. As I mentioned earlier, copyright laws can vary depending on the country. In the US, authors own the copyright to their work the moment they create it until 70 years after their death.

In India, too, copyright is automatic and is valid until 60 years after the death of the author. According to the *Handbook of Copyright Law* issued by the Indian government, "Acquisition of copyright is automatic, and it does not require any formality. However, certificate of registration of copyright and the entries made therein serve as *prima facie* evidence in a court of law with reference to dispute relating to ownership of copyright."[2]

The UK also has automatic copyright protection, with works protected for 70 years after the death of the author.

The UK Government website says, "You get copyright protection automatically—you don't have to apply or pay a fee. There isn't a register of copyright works in the UK." The website further goes on to say, "You can mark your work with the copyright symbol ©, your name, and the year of creation. Whether you mark the work or not doesn't affect the level of protection you have."[3]

Copyright is protected in other countries besides your home country through various international agreements.

Public Domain Content and Common Information

When copyright expires, a book reverts to the public domain, which means it now belongs to the public. Anyone can use literary works in the public domain without permission.

You might be surprised at some of the famous books that are in the public domain, which include *A Christmas Carol* by Charles Dickens, *The Adventures of Tom Sawyer* by Mark Twain, and *Gulliver's Travels* by Jonathan Swift. Many of the works of Jane Austen and William Shakespeare are also in the public domain, as the authors died over a hundred years ago.

Authors can also donate their work to the public domain by waiving their rights to copyright protection. Why would anyone ever do that? We might well ask. However, it's nevertheless true that several authors and photographers have donated their work to the public domain. It's also interesting to note that works issued by the US government are also in the public domain. However, other countries might have different laws regarding works created by their respective governments.

Some works do not have copyright protection. They include ideas, facts, business models, cooking recipes, titles, and domain names.

The US copyright law says, "In no case does copyright protection for an original work of authorship extend to any idea, procedure, process, system, method of operation, concept, principle, or discovery, regardless of the form in which it is described, explained, illustrated, or embodied in such work."[4]

The title of your book, too, can't be copyrighted. Neither can common facts, like the geographic location of a country, calendars, and dates of birth. However, this area can be a little tricky, as the actual arrangement of the facts can be copyrighted, but not the facts by themselves.

The purpose of this chapter is to help authors understand plagiarism, copyright laws, public domain information, and how it affects them. Sometimes, first-time authors haven't a clue about plagiarism, which means that they can unknowingly end up paying hefty fines and incurring penalties. So, knowing the fundamentals before you set about writing your book can save a lot of heartaches.

Notes

[1] "Plagiarize," Merriam-Webster (Merriam-Webster), accessed June 1, 2020, https://www.merriam-webster.com/dictionary/plagiarize.

[2] A Hand Book of Copyright Law, accessed June 1, 2020, http://copyright.gov.in/documents/handbook.html.

[3] Government Digital Service, "How Copyright Protects Your Work," GOV.UK (GOV.UK, November 18, 2015), https://www.gov.uk/copyright.

[4] "Ideas, Methods, or Systems," Ideas, Methods, or Systems § (2012)

CHAPTER 7

Storytelling Formulas

OVER THE LAST FEW years, I have helped publish many anthologies. Most of the chapters in the anthologies were written by everyday people and not by professional authors. The ones that I liked best were personal stories. The stories were enjoyable to read because the authors shared personal experiences. When we write about experiences that are close to our hearts, the reader feels the passion, and the work is more meaningful to us than a bland 'how-to' process.

Everybody's life stories are different. We might think that our stories are boring and that nobody wants to read them. But everyone's lives are different, and everyone has a different story to tell.

Throughout history, human beings as a species have been wired to both hear and tell stories. We love stories because they activate our brain cells and allow us to temporarily inhabit the author's experiences. Storytelling is that magic sauce that makes our content more interesting.

Our grandmothers have been telling us stories since time immemorial. Companies and brands occupy space in our minds by crafting stories related to their products and services, as a way of engaging our interest and encouraging us to buy from them. And, of course, the movies are all about stories. So, if we want our readers to read our books and take our advice, we must learn to tell stories that are both interesting and informative.

But...

What is a story? Is there a definition? According to the Cambridge Dictionary, a story is "a description, either true or imagined, of a connected series of events."[1]

There are many different kinds of stories. Some of them have a specific purpose. For example, some stories are designed to put us to sleep, while others are meant to keep us up at night. Think about a story that you like; it could be a story featured in a movie, a book, or even a sitcom. What did you like about it?

Was it funny, engaging, had an unexpected twist, or took you on a rollercoaster ride with lots of 'oohs' and 'aahs' along the way? I've put down my pointers on what I think makes a good story. These are things I've personally liked, but they could be something very different for you.

#1 Flow

The events should flow in a sequence so that each part of the story is connected to the other. If there's no connection between the sequence of events, there's a risk that the reader's flow of thought might break, and they may not grasp what is happening. The sequence of events needn't have to be in the order they occurred, it only needs to make sense to the audience and be connected in some way.

#2 A great beginning

The beginning of the story should immediately capture the reader's attention. We live in a world where we're competing for attention and are inundated with information. If we don't capture the reader's attention in the first five seconds, we can lose the reader quickly, which is why I recommend putting your best content at the beginning of the chapter.

#3 Personal

I tell people to talk about their personal experiences, but those experiences must be relevant to the objective of the chapter. Irrelevant stories with no inference or reason can cause the reader to drift away from the story's real objective. So, share personal experiences, but, at the same time, ensure that they are relevant to the context and objective of the chapter.

For example, talking about your most recent house purchase when the topic is food is irrelevant and not adding value to the reader. They didn't sign up to hear about the jacuzzi in your house.

I recommend digging into your past and searching for funny, entertaining, and challenging moments in your life. If you want to talk about an accomplishment, first talk about a challenge and how you overcame the challenge to achieve success. Talking about success without mentioning the problem you overcame could seem boastful. So, share personal stories in a manner that inspires your audience.

#4 Structure

When I wrote my first book, I had no clue about structure or storytelling formulas. I opened my word processor and just kept writing. Now, after more than a decade since writing my first book, I realize that storytelling can be broken down into a formula.

If we observe Hollywood movies, we see that most films have a structure. Those that don't are seldom a success.

Every romantic movie is almost the same; boy meets girl, they fall in love, then some misunderstanding or misfortune happens, but, in the end, they overcome it and magically come together.

The greatest authors throughout the centuries have similar patterns embedded in their work. Did they consciously use these patterns in their work, or was it subconscious? For instance, almost all of Shakespeare's plays have five acts. Many historians claim that Shakespeare did not divide his work into five acts, it was the authors who came much after him who edited his work into five acts.

Aristotle believed that any literary piece should have a beginning, middle, and an end. Did Aristotle believe that three acts form a whole? We don't know. However, several contemporary screenwriters have followed Aristotle's three-act formula as a standard practice. Kenneth Rowe, in his book, *Write That Play* says, "In recent years, by no rule, but in general practice, three [acts] has come more and more to be the standard."[2]

In this chapter, I'm going to discuss three popular storytelling formulas you can use in your book. There are several other storytelling formulas, but these are some of the most common and are also suitable when you're writing a non-fiction book.

Formula #1: The Three Act Structure

As I just mentioned, Aristotle was one of the early authors who believed a story needs to have a beginning, a middle, and an end. That's where we find the roots of the three-act structure.

Syd Field took a contemporary take on this three-act structure in his book *Screenplay,* published in 1979. He called the three acts—set-up, confrontation, and resolution. Each of these parts has a set of guidelines that writers can use to develop their stories.[3]

Now, let's look at the three-act structure in closer detail.

The First Act

The first act involves three parts: the set-up, the inciting incident, and the first plot point.

The set-up is where the author introduces the main characters, the world they live in, relationships, and everyday life. The set-up is followed by an inciting incident, where the main character is faced with a challenging situation that leads to the first plot point. The first plot point is a prelude to act two—this is where something dramatic happens and changes everything for the protagonist.

Act one is crucial because it sets the scene for the rest of the story. It's got to be tight and captivating for the reader to want to read the rest of the story.

Act Two: Confrontation

In act two, the protagonist deals with the problems and challenges that arise from the first act. Many things go wrong for the protagonist in act two, but they find a way to become a bigger, better person by building their character and learning new skills.

In real life, we're defined by the challenges we face, the experiences we've gone through, and the obstacles we've overcome. Think back over your life—what are the challenges you've faced? How did you overcome them? Who are the main characters who've shaped your life?

Fiction writers often believe that scenes ending in conflict make a story enjoyable. They intentionally create conflict between characters. The next time you watch a movie, try to observe this concept. You'll often see conflict between characters and a struggle to overcome them.

Conflict is a major part of real life, too. We rarely find solutions to our problems easily. We fight battles within ourselves. We can go through mental turmoil just making decisions, especially when it involves a life-changing incident.

Shopping to buy the right clothes, choosing a career, taking up a job, choosing the company to work for, choosing a wife or husband, getting divorced, or deciding what food to eat, are all decisions that create conflict in our minds. We want to be right. I'm not sure I know too many people who want to be wrong. In trying to be correct, we go through a lot of analysis in our minds.

Act two focuses on the struggles the protagonist goes through to achieve her goal.

Act Three: Resolution

In real life, we often struggle before we achieve our goal. If our goal is to be the CEO of a billion-dollar company, we go to college, get a degree, then an entry-level job, learn on the job for twenty years, network with the right people, showcase our expertise, and we may finally be rewarded with our dream job.

While act two is about the protagonist's struggles, act three is the part where the struggles reap the intended rewards, problems are resolved, and the protagonist either achieves her goal or fails. Then, the story concludes. However, the conclusion is not a simple or straightforward process.

The story has a climax, which is the highest possible point of tension. It's when the conflict from all corners comes together to create a dramatic high, where you think your head is going to explode, and the audience is perched on the edge of their seats desperate to know what will happen next.

The pre-climax precedes the climax, the point where you are going to build up the tension and gradually lead your audience to the resolution.

Finally, once your story reaches the climax, the maximum point of tension, you can't keep the audience there forever—you've got to bring them down. The denouement is when you end the story. It's the calm after the storm. You want to end your story, or even your corporate presentation, at its peak, but you cannot end it arbitrarily. Instead, you end it with a resolution to your conflict. It's best to keep the denouement short because the audience has gone through its maximum point of tension, and you don't want to bore them with a long ending.

So, to sum up, act three involves pre-climax, climax, and denouement. Get those right, and you will have an audience that is craving for more.

Formula #2: Before-After-Bridge

The Before-After-Bridge is one of my favorite formulas. It's where you show the readers a problem, then you ask them to imagine a world without that problem. Then, you offer a solution (or bridge) to where they are now to where they could be.

For example, say the reader's problem is that they are deeply in debt. They're struggling to make their mortgage payments every month, despite working two jobs. Now, ask the reader to imagine a world where they have no debt. Then, offer a solution to help them get out of debt.

The reader's point A is that they have excessive debt. Their point B is a world where they have no debt. Your solution should take them from point A to point B. The solution could be to write an instructional book titled, "How to go from debt up to your eyeballs to ZERO debt in less than a year." A non-fiction book can be a bridge (solution) to a problem. For first time authors, the Before-After-Bridge is one of the most straightforward structures to follow.

Formula #3: The Monomyth, or the Hero's Journey

Most popular cultures are obsessed with heroes. In the western world, we have Superman, Spiderman, and Batman. Irrespective of the culture you grew up in, it's likely that you've heard stories of people who have inspired you. Every culture loves its heroes (even if they're fictional) because they can do things that ordinary people may struggle to do but secretly wish they could. Our heroes have superpowers, unlimited courage, and are the saviors of the world. Call it hero worship, if you like.

Considering our age-old conditioning of hearing stories of heroes, it's not surprising that writers have come up with a popular formula called the Monomyth, or the Hero's Journey.

Joseph Campbell popularized the Hero Myth, which initially had no less than seventeen stages. In the 1990s, David Campbell and Phil Cousineau condensed it to eight stages; while Christopher Vogler's version featuring twelve stages was refined in his book *The Writer's Journey and* has proved the most popular.

The structure involves a hero who goes through a crisis (or a challenge), overcomes it, and comes back as a transformed person.

The hero leaves her ordinary world to venture into unknown territory, where she faces several challenges; through those challenges, they learn, evolve, and become a leader—ready to return and triumph.

For instance, in the Hindu mythological *Ramayana*, Lord Ram (Prince of Ayodhya) is exiled to the forest for fourteen years by his conniving stepmother. Meanwhile, his wife is abducted by the evil King Ravana. Lord Ram meets many interesting characters on his journey to rescue his wife. He creates an army of monkeys and bears, and ultimately kills Ravana and rescues his wife.

The Ramayana is an example of the hero's journey. Almost every culture around the world has similar stories.

If you plan on writing a book that follows the structure of the Hero's Journey, Christopher Volger's twelve-stage formula, as outlined below, is probably one of the most accessible contemporary versions.

Here are Vogler's twelve stages of the Hero's Journey:

Ordinary World

We introduce the hero and his world to our readers before his journey.

Call to Adventure

The hero is confronted with a challenge. It's a hint that his life is going to change.

Refusal of the Call

The hero initially refuses the call to adventure. He's either too scared or is just ignorant about the challenge.

Meeting with the Mentor

The hero decides to face the challenge and go on this adventure. But he is too inexperienced and lacks the wisdom of an experienced soul.

At this stage, the hero meets his mentor.

Crossing the First Threshold

The hero finally embarks on his adventure.

Tests, Allies, and Enemies

In this stage, the hero finds people who will either help him or drag him away from his mission.

Approach to the Inmost Cave

The hero digs deep and challenges his innermost beliefs, where he identifies whether he can or cannot succeed.

The Ordeal

The protagonist faces his biggest test so far. This is the stage where the inexperienced hero becomes an adult—if he survives!

Reward

After battling through the previous stages, the hero sees his reward.

The Road Back

The hero now tries to return to his ordinary world, but first must deal with the ramifications of stealing the reward.

The Resurrection

It's the final test for the hero, where the protagonist goes through near-death experiences; it's the climax of the story.

Return with the Elixir

Finally, the hero wins and gets to go home. He returns a different person—more mature and battle-hardened than when he started his adventure.

By using one of the formulas listed above, you can make your story more gripping, fun, and enticing for the reader. So, to sum up, while there are several storytelling formulas to choose from, those mentioned in this chapter are the most popular. It's best to choose a formula that suits your style and personality.

Notes

[1] "STORY: Meaning in the Cambridge English Dictionary," Cambridge Dictionary, accessed June 1, 2020, https://dictionary.cambridge.org/dictionary/english/story.

[2] Kenneth Thorpe Rowe, *Write That Play* (New York, NY: Funk and Wagnalls, 1968).

[3] Syd Field, *Screenplay: the Basics of Film Writing* (New York, NY: Delacorte Press, 1979).

CHAPTER 8

Research Methods

ONE OF MY EARLIEST books was *Insider Secrets to Raising Capital from Angel Investors*. When I wrote the book, I was by no means an expert on the topic. I realized that I needed to do some research—I had to find out from investors why they invested in certain companies and didn't invest in others. I contacted some investors and start-up founders and arranged to interview them, I asked them about their experiences in raising capital. They were happy to talk to me about it, and I was able to compile a book from their insights.

Of course, being an expert on a particular topic helps you enormously in writing a book. However, it's not possible to know everything about a topic. That's why it's so important to base our opinions on logic and reasoning, which come from making observations and doing research, analyzing the facts we gather, and getting different perspectives on similar issues. Often, no two experts agree on the same solution to a problem, so knowing different ways of achieving the same result gives your reader options.

Research involves expanding your information base, exploring new ideas, and organizing the information in a manner your reader can understand.

Research helps us support our arguments with facts. For example, in the chapter on plagiarism, I told the story of a promising author whose career was ruined by plagiarism. I heard about the story in the news when it happened, but I didn't remember the finer details. And that's okay when I'm sharing the story, say, during a conversation at a social event—it's not necessary in those circumstances to flesh out the minor details. However, when I realized it would make a good example for my readers warning them to avoid plagiarism in their writing, I had to do some research and check out the exact details of the event.

As non-fiction authors, we look for stories that support our statements and act as examples that educate our readers. Our memories are storehouses of hundreds of stories that we've heard from people, news outlets, books, and so on. Usually, we don't remember them accurately, so when we want to write about them and use them to illustrate a point, we need to do some research and ensure that we give readers as accurate and detailed an account as possible.

After helping several authors publish their books and having written many books myself, I was confident that writing a book about *how to write a book* would be a breeze. How wrong was I! Writing this book has been much harder than I initially thought it would be. I soon realized that I had been writing books out of pure instinct, with little organization. Most of my processes were at a sub-conscious level.

In this book, I've tried to use personal experiences as much as possible to give readers insight into the process of writing their first book. However, I've had to do much more research than I at first thought. I have had to dig into many sources to get the factual data required.

So, what exactly is research, and what does it entail for the author? The Merriam-Webster's dictionary defines research as the *"collecting of information about a particular subject."*[1]

There are primarily two kinds of research—primary and secondary.

Primary research involves collecting information directly from the source, which means contacting your source directly and asking questions. For example, if you were writing a book about marketing, it would be helpful to readers to have an insight from, say, an industry expert, or someone with first-hand experience about a specific event.

Another alternative is to organize a focus group and conduct surveys. For most non-fiction authors, interviews are perhaps the best way to get information from sources. I like interviews because they allow me to explore my chosen topic in more detail, which means that I often come away with new knowledge to incorporate in my book.

Secondary research involves collecting information from someone else's research. If someone has already done a survey that provides the information you want, there's no need to reinvent the wheel; you can simply quote information from that survey, provided you acknowledge the source. Private agencies, government organizations, and trade bodies all publish lots of useful information that is publicly available.

Secondary research can be the savior of the cash-strapped, first-time author, as primary research can incur costs, like travel expenses, that make primary research unaffordable. So, for example, when I need to know the number of books published in a year, it's impractical for me to get those numbers through primary research—I can't approach hundreds of original sources. But it's perfectly practical for me to get the data from secondary sources.

The research process starts with identifying the objectives of the research, which can be specific or open-ended.

The purpose of open-ended research is to give you detailed insights, fresh perspectives, and lead you to new places.

It involves asking open-ended questions, questions to which there are no simple yes or no answers but require a longer explanation. Open-ended questions are likely, therefore, to elicit much more information than closed ones.

For example, say you ask your interviewee, "Did you like being CEO?" Most likely, they'll simply answer, "Yes," and elaborate no further unless prompted. However, if you ask: "What was it you liked about being CEO?" They'll probably rattle away for several minutes, giving you useful insights and information that the closed question could never produce.

This is generally done in a one-on-one interview format where the interviewer asks open-ended questions, and the interviewee answers them in sentences and paragraphs. Usually, the interviewee is an industry expert with in-depth knowledge about the industry you're writing about.

Research is a significant part of writing a non-fiction book. However, I advise that you don't spend so much time researching that you don't put pen to paper: Try to write something every day. Eventually, you'll find the optimum balance between research and writing.

I've found the biggest challenge with secondary research to be authenticity. That's the reason why I recommend that you stay away from personal blogs whose content is subjective and may contain inaccurate information. Instead, focus your efforts on relevant information from credible sources, like trade journals, renowned industry publications, and published books.

Remember, it's crucial to collect accurate information. It's easy to find numbers and quotes on the internet, but they could be untrue and, therefore, unsuitable for inclusion in your book—you want to avoid misleading the reader with inaccuracies, which may also lead to damaging your reputation as a reliable source of information. I recommend being very careful when you're collecting information from unknown sources online. Imagine yourself to be an investigative journalist who must get her facts straight and learn to differentiate between fact, fiction, and opinions.

Today, the internet has made it easier than ever to access people who are experts in their field. The first thing you need to do is to make a list of the broad categories of people you want to interview. Then, list the objectives of the interview—try to be clear about the kind of information you want from your source. After you've made your list and have clarity on your objectives, the next step is to sign up on a website like HARO (helpareporterout.com).

HARO provides access to a vast database of expert sources on all sorts of topics. It's simple to sign up. All you need to do is list your query on HARO, and sources will pitch, saying why you should interview them for your book. In my experience, it's one of the easiest ways to find a source. You'll probably get several inquiries in response to your request for information but choose only the relevant ones. Then, set-up a time and schedule an interview. Before the interview, prepare a set of questions to ask. I suggest preparing at least ten open-ended questions. Remember, if the answer to a question is either yes or no, then it's probably a closed-ended question, which means you might not get all the information you want.

During the interview call, be polite, considerate, make the interviewee feel comfortable, and encourage them to give you detailed answers. Once they answer a question, try to encourage further conversation by picking up on specific points of their answer, so that you're adding to it, rather than just moving on to the next question.

For example, if the interviewee says, "I expect a salesperson to do at least four follow-ups." You could add to the answer by saying, "Do you think follow-ups help? I know a friend who is doing well in sales, but she never does a follow-up. Instead, she spends more time on newer customers. Is there ever a situation when not following up is recommended?"

If they answer, "In my experience, follow-ups always help irrespective of the industry. But I am aware that some salespeople don't follow-up because they are busy generating new leads."

You could further add, "In my business, I've seen that my conversions are better in the second or third follow-up. I've had close to zero conversions in my fourth follow-up."

By adding to an interviewee's answer, you are having a conversation rather than coming across as an interrogating robot.

Sometimes we tend to interrupt our interviewee before they complete their sentence. That could put them off, so always wait for the interviewee to finish answering.

The research process is also an excellent opportunity for you to get to know people who can help you promote your book once it's published. For example, well-known experts in your industry, celebrities, bestselling authors, and possible readers of your book can all be interviewed.

Even if you don't know someone, you can simply search for their email address online. You'll be surprised how many so-called experts have their emails listed online. Why not send out an exploratory email introducing yourself and asking them if you can speak to them for a few minutes? Some may not respond, but others will be delighted to be contacted; it's a game of numbers. Even if five out of a hundred people respond, that still presents several useful research opportunities and has cost you nothing but a little time.

Don't be surprised if people who you thought would be inaccessible turn out to be the easiest to access. The beauty of introducing yourself as an author is that you gain instant credibility. People respect authors and are more likely to respond to them.

Besides finding email addresses of experts online, you can also connect with sources on LinkedIn, which has the highest number of professionals online. The search feature on LinkedIn allows you to find people based on the size of the company, job title, company name, location, or even the specific school or university they attended. Interviewing sources can be a lot of fun. It's an opportunity to gain some great insights from experts in your industry and build valuable connections.

Remember—as I pointed out at the beginning of this chapter, none of us can know everything about a particular topic, and even experts can learn something new during the research process.

Notes

[1] "Research," Merriam-Webster (Merriam-Webster), accessed June 1, 2020, https://www.merriam-webster.com/dictionary/research.

CHAPTER 9

The Writing Process

IMAGINE, IT'S A COLD winter morning. You've made the important decision to write your first book. It's an exciting phase of your life. You open your word processor, and you have no clue where to start. It happens to all of us.

The idea of writing a book can be so overwhelming that it stays an idea for most people. It's not that many of these people don't have the necessary skills—I've seen people with excellent writing skills who've never written a book. And it's not because they don't want to, it's just that they don't have a process that works for them.

According to the Cambridge dictionary, the definition of process is, "A series of steps that you take to achieve a (desired) result."[1] The desired result for you, dear reader, is to produce a non-fiction book. Keeping this in mind, what are the series of steps that we must take to write a good non-fiction book?

When I wrote my first book, I'm not sure if I had a conscious process. I wrote sporadically. I didn't take the time to plan and structure my thoughts. If I had a process, I might have written a better book faster and felt less overwhelmed. The purpose of a writing process is that it breaks down the massive project of writing a book into smaller, simpler steps.

I like to break down the writing process into four parts—planning, writing your first draft, rewriting, and editing.

Step 1: Planning

The first part of the writing process is planning. In the planning stage, the writer creates an outline of the book, which includes a list of chapters and an outline for each chapter. So, step 1 is creating a list of chapters.

We've discussed how to create a list of chapters in the Book Plan chapter of this book. Once you read it, you can write a list of chapters and move on to the next step in the process—Outlining.

Step 2: Writing an Outline for Each Chapter

In this step, I write the basic points I want to cover in each chapter. One of the biggest challenges for an author is clarity. When we start writing a book, there are so many decisions to make. What chapters to include? Which ones to exclude? What content should go in each chapter? You'll probably find that your mind is suddenly filled with thousands of questions, all clamoring for an answer.

The antidote to this confusion is to create a chapter outline. By doing this, I'm organizing my thoughts. The outline allows me to clarify in my mind all the points that I want to include in my chapter.

Initially, I didn't like the process of outlining. I thought it would stifle my thoughts. But I have changed my opinion over the years, and I now enjoy the process of outlining. It gives structure to my chapters, and I find having to focus on one idea or a single paragraph at one time to be less overwhelming.

Besides adding structure to your writing, it also acts as a cue or trigger to unlock the subconscious thoughts that may be hidden somewhere inside your brain.

I start out by first making a list of all the essential points I want to cover in my chapter outline. Let's say I choose to cover ten separate points in my chapter—then I need to only write about 200 to 300 words per point, and my chapter is done. This planned approach makes handling several ideas less overwhelming by breaking down a large process into easily manageable smaller steps. As Warren Buffett says, "I don't look to jump over seven-foot bars; I look around for one-foot bars that I can step over."[2] It's like saying, I want to break down the book writing process into a series of one-foot bars rather than seven-foot bars.

It's helpful to think of it like this: Imagine someone asked you to write 60,000 words about something—you would probably be horrified—how on earth could you write that much? But what if I asked you to write a paragraph of 300 words? That sounds much more achievable than writing 60,000 words, doesn't it? Of course, it does! Yet by writing 300 words about 200 ideas; over time, your 60,000-word book is done. It's like eating a watermelon—we don't swallow it all at once, but we eat it bit by bit.

Most experienced writers will tell you that an author's despair is the blank page. When we see a blank page, we don't know what to write. Some writing workshops give attendees writing prompts and ask them to write anything related to the prompt that comes to their mind—a prompt acts as a catalyst that sparks the writer's imagination. Even when I write an outline, I don't have a clue where my writing is going to take me. Sometimes, I go into territories I'd never imagined before. An outline acts as a prompt that sparks new ideas. It is that little push that unlocks our sub-conscious thoughts.

That's why I like to outline my chapter before I start writing, and I strongly recommend that you do the same. If you talk to ten authors, each one of them will probably give you a different process. Every author has her own method that they have developed over time. You may have to experiment and be flexible when trying to find an outlining process that works best for you.

Here is one process for you to try:

First, pick the chapter you want to outline.

Then, write the primary objective of that chapter. List just one objective. If you have more than one objective, consider breaking it up into two or more chapters. Then, write the main points the reader needs to know to achieve that objective.

Every chapter has certain basic characteristics—one of them is the 'hook,' which entices the reader into reading the rest of the chapter.

The hook can be a shocking statement or a fact. It can be, for example, a personal story of grief, happiness, or anger. I like happy stories. However, stories filled with sadness, anger, and misery attract more readers than stories of joy, perhaps because we want to see our heroes challenged and overcome hardships to achieve their objective. Bad news spreads faster than good news, which is the reason why mass media is filled with bad news.

If you watched the movie *Hangover*, you might remember that in the first scene, a character walks into the restroom and sees a tiger in there. He's shocked, and so is the audience. This demonstrates that you don't need to explain everything in chronological order. Instead, you start your chapter with the most exciting paragraph. If the first line is boring, the reader probably won't bother to read on. That's the reason why the hook is the first paragraph of your chapter. You can even go back and write the hook once you've completed writing your chapter.

A basic chapter template I use when writing and structuring my non-fiction book is—*What?*, *Why?* and *How?*, followed by a *Conclusion*. I'll explain this template in more detail below.

Definition (What?)

In my chapter outline, I like to add a definition of the topic I'm going to cover in the chapter. First, I write some of the basic points

I want to talk about. Let's say, for example, I want to talk about outlining—then I'll first explain what it is. My definition is the *What* aspect of the topic. Sometimes, I skip the definition and write a basic discussion of the topic.

The Why?

After I explain what I am going to cover in the chapter, I tell the reader why they need this information. For example, if I used the question "What is outlining?" to head up my definition in the previous paragraph, I can then explain to the reader the reasons why they should create an outline before writing a chapter. This process helps to impress upon the reader the reasons why it is so important to do a specific thing, in this case, to write a chapter outline, and how it will benefit their writing process.

The How?

After covering the *Why* aspect of the topic, I then tackle the main topic of the chapter, explaining the *How* of doing something or the best way to do it.

Once I am done with explaining the *How*, I then write a conclusion or closing statement for the chapter. It can be a summary of the chapter or a callback from the hook. For instance, if your hook was a question, then you can provide a short summary of the answer to that question. The conclusion is your opportunity to make a final statement to the reader. In the body of the chapter, you are presenting your arguments, and at the end of the chapter, you are stamping your authority on it by saying, "I believe this statement is true because..."

Some authors like to add a transition to the next chapter at the end of the previous one. This often happens in, for example, sitcoms, where the scriptwriter or director creates a little bit of tension or mystery at the end of an episode to entice viewers to tune in for the next one to discover the outcome. You want your reader to turn the page and keep reading. As readers, we all remember times when we've said, "I'm just going to read for an hour before I go to bed," then finding ourselves still awake six hours later, having read the whole book from cover to cover. As writers, that's what we should be aiming to do for our readers—ensuring that our books have a nice flow so that they struggle to put the book down.

For me, the initial chapter outline is only a writing guideline. If a new idea pops up in my head, I simply go back to my initial outline and update it to include new ideas.

Here's an example of an outline I used for this chapter:
Objective of the Chapter: Explain the writing process
Definition of a process: Why do we need a writing process?
Mention the parts of the writing process
Then, explain each part in detail
Write a conclusion.

As you can see, my outline is only a basic list of points I wanted to cover in this chapter. You'll notice that I haven't gone into a lot of detail. That's because, at this stage, I simply want to develop a basic structure and work through the steps involved. However, there's no reason why you can't add more detail to your outline if you choose. But don't make it too complicated, or you might lose sight of your chapter goal.

Here's the template of the outlining process we've just discussed:
Chapter Hook: Shocking statement, question, anything to catch your reader's attention
Definition: The 'What' of your topic. Define your topic.
The Why: Why does the reader need it? Why is it important?
The How: How to achieve the objective of the chapter?
Conclusion: Closing statement, summary, a callback to the hook, or a transition to the next chapter.

We've now finished creating the initial outline that forms your framework. At this stage, you should have a clear understanding of the benefits of creating an outline and how to do it.

Now it's time to move on to the next step of the writing process.

Step 3: Writing Your First Draft

During this phase of writing, the most important thing is to just write. Don't pause and reread what you've written, don't try to judge your writing, and try to resist the urge to edit while you write. I like to call this the dumping stage, because you are dumping your thoughts into your word processor. There will be plenty of time to clean up and reorganize your writing later during the rewriting and editing phase. So, for now, focus on quantity without worrying too much about the quality of your words.

Choose the time and place where you'll write.

Stick to that schedule every single day.

For example, if you choose to write at 6 a.m. sitting at your desk in the living room, then do that every day. You might find that the best time to write is usually as soon as you wake up, as that is when your energy levels are at their highest. Or, you might discover that you work best in the afternoon or are a 'night owl' who performs better later in the day. Once you start writing regularly, you'll soon discover what routine works for you.

Initially, it'll take commitment to stick to a schedule. However, it won't be long before that commitment becomes a habit—and good habits create good outcomes.

Once you set up your schedule and stick to it for six months, you'll find that you have enough content for your book. That's already a great achievement.

But now comes the bad news—writing a book is hard work. It requires a lot of writing, rewriting, and editing. Here's what two highly successful authors have to say about writing a book:

Michael Crichton wrote, "Books aren't written—they're rewritten. Including your own. It is one of the hardest things to accept, especially after the seventh rewrite hasn't quite done it."[3]

William Zinsser, author of the book On Writing Well, wrote, "Writing is hard work. A clear sentence is no accident. Very few sentences come out right the first time or even the third time. Remember this in moments of despair. If you find that writing is hard, it's because it is hard."[4]

After completing the writing phase, most authors realize that their book is unorganized. They may find that they've repeated the same sentences or words several times, and their writing may lack structure.

Even if the author has prepared an outline, it's not uncommon to drift away from it and take a dramatically different path. So, the first step in the rewrite process is to rewrite the outline. Many authors realize that it's much easier to write an outline the second time around after they have finished writing the chapter.

Once the author has rewritten the outline, the next step is to trim the content, which means going back to the content to delete any words, phrases, or sentences that you've repeated or are unnecessary, or simply don't make sense. This is your chance to reorganize the content to ensure that it's in line with the structure laid out in your outline.

For instance, you'll probably find that some content is not in the right place—perhaps it belongs towards the end of the chapter or even in a different chapter altogether? As you read back what you've written, you might decide that some content would fit better at the beginning of the chapter or in the middle, and so on.

Once you've organized your content, it's time to go through each sentence to see if they need restructuring to make its meaning clearer, easier to read, or even just look better on the page.

Try to shorten long sentences. Consider breaking up long sentences into two or more sentences, if necessary.

At this point, your aim should be to get better at writing—it's not necessary to be perfect. Once you've completed reconstructing your sentences to your satisfaction, it's time to find if there are any knowledge gaps in the book. Certain chapters of the book may be incomplete because you lack knowledge on a particular issue. If you find that this is the case, you may have to do a little research to fill in the gap, or perhaps find a helpful expert who is happy to add their expertise in exchange for a mention or a quote in your book.

You can find experts to interview on a site called HARO (www.helpareporterout.com). It's free. All you need to do is signup, place your query, and interested people can get in touch with you.

Once you complete the rewriting process, the next step is the editing and proofreading of your book.

There are two choices here: You can do the editing yourself or find a good editor to edit the book for you. In my experience, most writers are not good editors of their own work. Plus, when you've looked at your text for a long time, you are likely to miss small errors, like typos and punctuation mistakes. I highly recommend finding a good editor to edit the book for you, although it will cost you some money.

Most first-time authors starting out don't have a budget to hire an editor and must get creative about finding ways of getting their work edited. For example, you could try swapping a skill or item you have in exchange for editing services. But before that, let's have a look at the different types of editing.

There are primarily four types of editing: developmental editing, copy editing, line editing, and proofreading.

Developmental editing refers to the big picture. It happens early on in the editing process. The developmental editor will look into the structure of the book, the idea, its marketability, the organization of chapters, and ensure that it is consistent with the theme and message of the book. This process starts in the book planning stage.

Copy editing focuses on the text, grammar, sentence construction, and the mechanics of language. The copy editor's job is to make the author's manuscript look more professional through the correct usage of language. Many of us use slang when we talk, and it carries over to our writing. For example, although I had been writing for several years, it wasn't until I found a professional editor that I discovered that I was making mistakes I didn't even know were mistakes.

A copy editor can spot errors that writers believe to be correct. Plus, having a qualified expert have a look at your work is a nice way of getting a second opinion to see if you're on the right track.

While *copy editing* focuses on mechanics, *line editing* focuses on style. Line editing is more of an art than a science. It's subjective because the line editor is making your text more fun and enjoyable for the reader. We've often picked up a book that has interesting content but isn't an enjoyable read because of the author's poor writing style.

So, to sum up, *copy editing* focuses on the correctness of language, while *line editing* focuses on style.

Proofreading is the final stage of editing. It is done after line editing and copy editing. The proofreader's job is to check for spelling, grammatical, and punctuation errors.

There's one more important part of the editing process to go through before your book is ready for its final pre-publication checks—it's called *fact-checking*.

In a non-fiction book, fact-checking is very important, especially if you reference a lot of data. The job of a fact-checker is to report any inaccuracies in facts. For example, a historian writing about a war writes that 5000 people were killed, when, in fact, only fifty people died, then that is inaccurate and misleading to the reader.

That is the type of thing your fact-checker should bring to your attention. Another example is the common tendency to quote people inaccurately, which is something that a good fact-checker will alert you to.

Once you've completed writing, editing, proofreading, and fact-checking your content, you may want to reorganize your chapters once more, repeating the restructuring process that you began earlier on to bring your chapters in line with your original outline.

When you're comfortable with the sequence of your chapters, it's time to do one final round of editing before you hand your completed book over to a professional editor or your publisher. Remember, your aim is to offer a polished product that is a pleasure to read and ensures the best possible experience for your reader.

In the next chapter, we'll discuss *self-editing* and the best ways to do it.

Notes

[1] "PROCESS: Meaning in the Cambridge English Dictionary," Cambridge Dictionary, accessed June 1, 2020, https://dictionary.cambridge.org/dictionary/english/process.

[2] Jill Schlesinger, "Another Great One-Liner from Warren Buffett," CBS News (CBS Interactive, November 4, 2009), https://www.cbsnews.com/news/another-great-one-liner-from-warren-buffett-03-11-2009/.

[3] Thomas Clark, "174 Tips From Bestselling Writers," *Writer's Digest*, September 1986.

[4] William Knowlton. Zinsser, *On Writing Well: the Classic Guide to Writing Nonfiction* (New York, NY: Collins Reference, 2005).

CHAPTER 10

How to Self-Edit?

IMAGINE, YOU'VE WRITTEN FOR over 200 hours in the last six months. You have over 60,000 words of content. You're not sure if it's gibberish or the greatest piece of work you've ever written until today. Now, what do you do with it? Do you ship it off to a professional editor, or do you edit it yourself?

A good editor can turn your manuscript into the best possible version of your work. However, if the content is unorganized and messy, it will be much harder for an editor, however good they are, to get it to a good enough standard for publication.

In my career as a publisher, I've seen manuscripts that are terrible even after three rounds of edits. That's because the original was awful. The editor may have tried their best to fix it, but there is only so much even the best editor can do. If you want to produce a manuscript that is as close to perfection as possible, you must learn to self-edit before a professional editor lays eyes on it.

A trainer I know sent me a copy of his book. I was excited to see what he'd written. However, when I picked it up to read it, I found grammatical errors in the title of the book, as well as errors on the back cover, and throughout the whole book. The grammatical errors made it difficult and annoying to read, so I put the book away and didn't bother to finish reading it.

Wonderful books don't happen by accident. It usually takes several rewrites and edits before the reader sees the final version.

Self-editing is an essential part of the writing process. Some of you might be wondering if you still need to use a professional editor if you are self-editing your book. The answer is, yes. A good professional editor can spot errors that you've missed. Plus, they'll be able to, for instance, give your suggestions on how to improve your sentence construction. Sometimes, when we write, we assume things in our minds and tend not to complete our thoughts. That can mean that a point or argument we're trying to convey is not complete. There might be a crucial part missing; an editor will pick up on that and draw your attention to it, asking questions that will help you to fill in the missing pieces.

What Is Self-Editing?

Self-editing is the process of polishing your writing in order to make the reader's experience as enjoyable as possible. It includes things like correcting typos, grammatical errors, restructuring sentences, ensuring clarity of meaning, making the writing feel more active, improving flow and style, and anything else that guarantees your book will be an enjoyable read.

Guidelines to Self-Editing—What to Look For?

Many great authors advice that you should take a break before editing your work. They say that it allows the work to marinate in our minds so that we can emotionally detach ourselves from the writing process and take a step back to look at it more objectively. Editing involves deleting sentences, and it can be painful to remove sentences that we took so much time to write and put together.

Bestselling writer Stephen King likes to take six weeks off before he attempts to edit his work. King uses the analogy of a forest to say, "When you write a book, you spend day after day scanning and identifying the trees. And, when you're done, you have to step back and look at the forest. And after you've spent countless hours writing the book, and you need to trim the trees, you are forbidden to feel depressed about them or to beat up on yourself. Screw-ups happen to the best of us."[1]

After those comforting words, I'd like to share with you the simple process I use to self-edit my work:

Step 1: Reorganize the Chapters and the Content

During the rewriting process, you may have rewritten your outline. In the editing phase, you have an opportunity to go back and reorganize any chapters that feel out of place, so that they eventually flow in a logical sequence. You can also delete any chapters that no longer seem a good fit for your book. You can always file away the deleted content and repurpose it somewhere else in the book or use it in another book. I find it useful to save the deleted material in a separate folder.

Step 2: Delete Unnecessary Words and Sentences

I remember a while ago seeing a stand-up comic, who said, "Brevity is hard." That's true, yet a good writer tries to convey their meaning to their readers in as few words as possible—they just have to be the right words.

So, one of the first things you're going to do when you start to edit is remove any unnecessary and superficial words.

In his book *On the Art of Writing*, Sir Arthur Quiller-Crouch tried to convey what it takes to be a good writer by saying that you must "Murder your darlings."[2]

When we write, we often don't notice that we tend to repeat ourselves, using the same sentences by paraphrasing them, or two sentences when only one is needed to get our meaning across.

For example, look at the sentences below:

Success, to me, is making a difference in people's lives.

Transforming people's lives makes me feel successful.

Don't these two sentences mean the same thing? The writer is repeating themselves, just saying the same thing in two different ways. The second sentence isn't required because it's not adding anything new.

The biggest advantage of being a writer is that we can edit our work. We can clean up the content by removing excess material, which will help make our sentences tighter, more compact, and more meaningful to the reader.

Finding better words to express our meaning is another aspect of self-editing that we have control over. Can you replace a word with another word that sounds better or is more meaningful than the original? Does the original word do justice to the idea you're trying to convey? I don't believe that using fancy or complicated words that are difficult to understand is helpful to the reader. A book is not the place where an author should showcase her excellent vocabulary. My recommended formula is to keep it simple so that even a seven-year-old will understand what you're trying to say.

If your audience needs a dictionary to understand your writing, that's a sign that you've used too many complicated words.

Unnecessary words and phrases, like *definitely, for sure, very,* and *only*, can often be deleted. Using lots of adjectives can also be annoying. In India, I've seen people use the word 'only' when it is entirely irrelevant. In the US, people tend to use the word 'awesome' more frequently than is desirable. Everything in the world cannot always be awesome but can also be fantastic, beautiful, and pleasant.

Step 3: Shorten Sentences

Long sentences are harder to read. If you find that you tend to write long sentences that become confusing as a result, try breaking them up. Split them up into two, or even three shorter, punchier sentences.

You'll find that they are much more effective.

Sometimes, I see writers trying to do too much in a sentence. They try hard to cram all their thoughts into a single sentence, which can lead to them being rambling and hard to follow. I've found that a good rule of thumb to remember is: One sentence equals one thought.

Step 4: Rewrite Sentences in Active Voice

Writing coaches will tell you to write in active voice as much as possible. Even in college, I remember points being deducted for writing in passive voice.

But what is the difference between the two?

Take a look at these two sentences:

"Robert punched George."

"George was punched by Robert."

The first one is written in active voice. Robert is the subject, punched is the verb, and George is the object. When the subject is doing the action on the object, that's active voice.

What about the second sentence? In this sentence, George becomes the subject and Robert the object. The subject is passive and not doing anything. So, it's in passive voice.

So, why should we try to write using active voice?

Let's look at those two sentences again:

"Robert punched George."

"George was punched by Robert."

The meaning is the same. But which one sounds better? Does the one with active voice sound better? Or does the passive voice sound better?

Sentences in active voice add impact to the conversation. They're dynamic and make the subject look like they are actively doing something to move the conversation forward.

Writing in passive voice is not wrong. Sometimes, it's necessary. But there are some negatives aspects to it for writers. For example, sentences in passive voice are longer. Secondly, it just doesn't have the impact of passive voice. It turns an exciting moment into a dull one. Plus, passive voice can stifle the meaning we're trying to convey, and unnecessarily complicate sentence structure.

Let's take another example:
I bought a bunch of roses. My girlfriend loved it.
Both of these sentences are in active voice.
Now, let's write them in passive voice to see how they sound.
The roses were bought by me. They were loved by my girlfriend.
Isn't it evident that active voice sounds so much better? It's shorter, snappier, more direct, as well as easier to understand?

There will be times when it's impossible to write in active voice. That's fine, just try to make the best use of active voice whenever you can—it will make your writing voice sound much better!

Step 5: Check for Grammar

As a writer, you don't need to be an expert on grammar. If you can write at high school English level, then you'll be fine. Just stick to the basics outlined in this book—that's all you need. Of course, it's helpful to learn as much as you can about the basics of grammar, but you'll probably pick up a lot of that as you continue writing, especially if you find a good editor. I don't think my grammar is that brilliant, but I know enough to self-edit my books effectively. I also read lots of books and articles, which means I'm brushing up my grammar skills all the time.

One of the advantages that modern writers have is today's technology—we're so lucky to have so much software designed to make our lives as authors easier. For instance, you don't have to be the world's greatest speller, because online tools like "Grammarly" can catch even your most glaring errors and typos. Sadly, software is not always 100% accurate, so you'll still need to know a bit about grammar when using them. In my experience, it's unwise to blindly accept the software's suggestions in all cases—it's prudent to check it yourself.

Step 6: Check for Typos

If you've been lucky enough to have something you've written published, you'll know that sinking feeling when you're smilingly reading through it—and a typo leaps out from the page, ruining the experience. This can happen even if you've employed an editor. The typo, or more correctly, the typographical error, is the bane of a writer's life; "the" ends up written as "teh," "receive" comes out as "recieve," "they" reads "there," even though you checked and double-checked before submitting the piece. We've all spotted typos in magazines, newspapers, and, more commonly, in blog posts. However, the better the quality of those books, magazines, and newspapers, the fewer typos there'll be. Blogs written by amateur writers usually contain many more typos than they should. A few typos may go unnoticed by the novice reader, but when there are too many of them, they become annoying for the reader.

Typos include spelling mistakes, omissions, and punctuation errors. But with modern software like "Grammarly," and a much-improved MS Word's built-in spell check, it's now much easier to spot typos than ever before.

Step 7: Fact-Checking

The world is filled with information and disinformation, especially in the era of "fake news." That's why it's essential to check the reputation of the person or institution sharing the information. We see people share information on social media all the time, but how many of them have bothered to check whether their source is trustworthy or not?

As authors, we should be skeptical of every piece of information. If the facts or statistics are part of your secondary research, take the time to track down the original source—then make sure you cite it in your book.

The best thing is to avoid quoting "facts" drawn from blogs and social media posts. Better to spend your time researching more authentic sources, like government agencies, published books, and research reports from reputed institutions, where you can be sure the facts are reliable.

The purpose of fact-checking is to ensure that the information you're presenting to your readers is accurate. In the era of Google, readers are more informed than ever before, and it usually only takes a few clicks to figure out if your information is accurate or not.

It's necessary to fact-check quotes from people, statistics, and any information that is factual rather than mere opinion.

When I'm writing a non-fiction book, I like to highlight all the sentences in my book that need fact-checking. Even if you hire a fact-checker, you want them to be checking for any information you may have missed. That's why a double-check is always beneficial.

Step 8: Plagiarism Check

Whenever we research something for a book we're writing, it's easy to copy someone else's content unknowingly. It's even possible for us to explain a thought in the same words as another author without realizing we're doing it. That's something that good writers need to avoid. So, it's imperative to do a plagiarism check. Tools like "Copyscape" and "Grammarly" can perform plagiarism checks for you and save you from any embarrassment—or lawsuits.

Step 9: Beta Readers

Get a friend or someone from your writing group to read your manuscript. It's good to get feedback from someone else. When you've spent months writing something, it's tough to step back and look at it objectively. It's hard to be one's own critic. Getting somebody else to read your book means getting some valuable critical feedback that can ultimately help to make your book a better read. If you look online, you'll find many writer's groups where writers support each other by reading and offering critiques of each other's work. Why not join one and take advantage of that?

Step 10: Knowing When It's Done

The hardest thing for an author is to know when their book is finished. If you're self-publishing, it's entirely under your control to choose when to publish.

Some authors publish their book before it's properly done. My team and I come across many self-published books that seem half-baked and are a terrible experience for the reader. Other writers get themselves stuck in a perfectionist mode of paralysis analysis; they're constantly seeking feedback and making changes to their manuscript and end up never publishing their book. It would be nice to be perfect, but perfection doesn't exist.

Let's say that, if you've done two rewrites, three rounds of self-editing, and two rounds of editing by a professional editor, then it's time to hit publish.

If you follow the guidelines outlined here, you'll be fine.

Will there still be errors in the book?

Probably. As already discussed, not every tiny error will be caught. So, don't fret about it, just know that you've done your best to keep the number of errors as close to zero as possible.

Self-editing is a process that's carried out prior to sending your manuscript to a professional editor. You polish your script yourself and do everything you can to make it the best possible version, before finally handing it over to a professional editor, who will then make it even better.

In the meantime, keep working on your writing and editing skills. Remember, the goal is not to be perfect, but to be better than you were yesterday.

Notes

[1] Stephen King, *On Writing: a Memoir of the Craft* (New York, NY: Scribner, 2010).

[2] Arthur Thomas Quiller-Couch, *On the Art of Writing* (Mineola, NY: Dover Publications, 2006).

CHAPTER 11

How to Hire an Editor?

GOOD EDITING CAN DRAMATICALLY transform your content. It makes the writing flow and ensures that it's well-organized so that it's more enjoyable to read. A second pair of eyes can usually spot errors that the author may have missed. Sometimes, we make certain errors because we don't even know that they are errors. So, hiring a good editor not just cleans up our writing, but also teaches us new things.

Obviously, as with everything in life, there are good, average, and bad editors out there.

I prefer to work with an editor I respect and admire. Fortunately, since I'm in the publishing industry, my network of editors is pretty good. I also take up editing work for clients who are looking for editing services but don't want to spend time finding an editor themselves.

Over the years, I've seen even the best editors make mistakes. As they say, nobody is perfect, but you need to find someone as close to perfect as possible.

Before hiring an editor, it's essential to first identify what type of editor is needed for your project. As mentioned in the chapter on writing processes, there are basically four types of editors—developmental editors, copy editors, line editors, and proofreaders. Each of these types of editors will get involved at different stages in readying your book for publication. For instance, a developmental editor comes in at the early stages of the book production process, while the copy editor and line editor follow on from that, with the proofreader coming in at the final stages.

Since hiring four different types of editors is likely to be too expensive for a first-time author, it's best to practice becoming better at self-editing, then hire a copy editor with experience of line editing who can also proofread your book.

I believe first-time authors should invest in a writing coach rather than hiring a developmental editor until they start earning an income from their writing. A good coach can teach you the ropes of developmental editing. In the initial stages, you should try to be frugal in your approach and develop your self-editing skills as much as possible. This will save you time and money in the long run.

Once you've identified the kind of editor you need, the next step is to decide the skills you need them to have.

Qualities to Look for in an Editor

Here are my suggestions on what to look for:

#1 Knowledge about Grammar

Try to pick an editor whose grammar is perfect, and can identify grammatical flaws in your writing and correct them. The English language has specific rules for grammar and punctuation, which is important to get right. Some authors break these rules and get away with it because they know the rules and how and when to break them to good effect. Not many of us are specialists in grammar, but a good editor should have impeccable grammar and be able to fix even the most complex grammatical errors.

Fixing grammatical errors is one of the primary jobs of a copy editor. If you have a limited budget, then hiring a copy editor could be the solution. As you keep growing as a writer and start earning an income from your writing, you will probably be able to afford a line editor. Editing costs can sometimes spiral out of control, so budget your costs for editing appropriately and negotiate with your editor to keep your costs low.

#2 Attention to Detail

Editing is rather like ferreting out needles from a haystack. As the old saying goes, "The devil is in the details." When you clean up small errors throughout your writing, you'll be surprised how suddenly it can become a "clean" masterpiece. As an author, it's wonderful to see how little things can make a big difference to the quality of your writing and, therefore, to the end product.

Try reading a bestselling book with the eye of an editor, and you'll probably notice a few errors. That's because no book is 100% error-free. However, it's best to ensure the number of errors in every book is kept to a minimum. Ideally, the error rate should be below 1%. Anything more than 1% can get annoying for the reader, as it interferes with their concentration and makes reading less enjoyable.

When reading is no longer a pleasure, readers are likely to toss your book aside and move on to another book. That's why it's best to choose a copy editor who is detail oriented and can go through every detail of your manuscript and spot the errors that the average reader may not even notice.

#3 Good Communication Skills

I once hired an editor who communicated in monosyllables, so most of her replies consisted of one or two words. Plus, she came across as rude and arrogant. I found it hard even to have a conversation with her. That's why I recommend finding an editor who is an excellent communicator and is happy to explain her methodology and give you useful suggestions as to how you can improve your writing. For example, when you think something you've written is right, but the editor says it needs changing, then she must be able to clearly explain why, so that you can avoid making the same mistake again, saving both time and money.

#4 Consistent

Good writing is about consistency. A good editor should be able to identify any inconsistencies and fix them. But, be warned—not all editors are consistent. However, the good ones will work hard to ensure that your book is consistent in terms of styling, grammar, and British/American English, amongst a host of other things.

#5 Organized

As an organized person myself, I prefer to work with well-organized editors. Being organized means putting things in order, for instance, ensuring there is a home for files, that there are files for separate things so that you can access the information you need quickly without wasting time. In the final analysis, you'll find that it's not so much about how much time you have, but how well you manage it. Editors should make optimum use of their time. I don't like working with editors who appear clueless because their minds, and probably their desks, are so cluttered that they don't remember half of the things they've said or done.

These are some of the qualities I recommend looking for in an editor.

Where to Find an Editor?

You can search for an editor in three main places—job listings and freelance portals, marketplaces, and agencies.

Step-By-Step Process for Hiring an Editor

Step 1: Type of Editor

The first step in hiring an editor is to decide what type of editor you need. Most authors, more often than not, require a good copy editor. Developmental and line editors are also helpful, but it might be a little expensive for a first-time author to hire them all. It's important to be careful with your budget when you are starting your writing career, as it's possible to lose a lot of money very fast. I've heard many authors suggest that hiring a developmental editor and a line editor early on in the process is helpful. Still, I wouldn't recommend that approach when you're just starting out. I would suggest it's probably going to be more useful to spend the money on hiring a writing coach, who can help you grow your skills, before going on a costly shopping spree hiring developmental and line editors.

Step 2: Budget

Once you've decided on the type of editor you need, the next step is to determine how much you're prepared to spend on editing. Be realistic about the budget you can afford. Editing is the most expensive part of the book production process. You might be lucky and find a good editor with affordable rates. However, if you want the editing to be comprehensive and complete, then you should consider hiring an agency where your manuscript will go through several rounds of editing before you lay eyes on it.

However, if you're confident that your command of grammar is excellent, then consider hiring an intern, or a friend, who you know to be a good editor as this can dramatically reduce your costs.

It's a good idea to ask any potential editors to provide samples of their work before hiring them. Most reputable editors will have a portfolio of examples that you can view.

Step 3: Agency or Freelancer?

Agencies have certain advantages over freelancers because they usually have several editors, proofreaders, and account managers available to work on clients' projects. Account managers should be well-versed in customer service because they handle client's accounts and act as the interface between clients and editors. Account managers ensure that projects are completed according to specifications and within the agreed-upon time.

In contrast, freelancers are individuals, and there is only so much that a single individual can take on in terms of scale. Generally, an editing project requires multiple sets of eyes scrutinizing it at different stages in the process, which means that agencies offer a higher chance of ensuring that your manuscript is as error-free as possible.

However, the upside of hiring a freelancer is that you may be able to negotiate a reasonable price, as you're dealing with the individual directly. The downsides could include a lack of accessibility or delays in meeting your deadlines because the freelancer is handling multiple projects.

Agency benefits include the provision of a project manager well-versed in customer service and the knowledge that several editors are going to be covering your project, which means a better quality final product. Moreover, project managers and editors are experienced and can usually provide you with valuable feedback.

If you decide to go with an agency, try to choose one you trust, perhaps via a personal recommendation, and one that you can be reasonably sure is run by good people who are experienced at what they do.

My agency helps authors with editing, designing, typesetting, and author websites. We also assist authors in getting their books published on Amazon, as well as with several other online and offline retailers. This provides an excellent solution for writers who want to get on with writing, and don't want to deal with editors and designers directly. We do all that for them through our hassle-free service. You can visit our website www.publishedge.com for more details.

Step 4: List of Job Listing Sites or Agencies

Now you know what to look for in an editor; the next step is to make a list of job listing sites or agencies. Alternatively, you could find a marketplace and search for freelancers there.

Step 5: Shortlisting

Once you've made a list of agencies and freelancers, bearing in mind the earlier tips on what sort of editor you need and what skills they should have, come up with a shortlist of your top three candidates. Go ahead and contact each of them, and see who you feel most comfortable with:

Are they friendly? Do they have the experience you need and seem genuinely interested in your project? Do they have a good grasp of what's required? Are they open to negotiating on price? If you've established these things to your satisfaction, then ask each one of them to give you a quote. And, select the one that seems to best suit your needs.

Step 6: Negotiate Price

The final step in the process is to agree on the price, the terms of payment, and the timeline. Some agencies can ask 100% of the entire payment upfront, while others, for example, could ask for 50% of the total cost upfront, 25% after the first edit, and 25% after the second edit.

If you're not sure you want to tie yourself into a lengthy contract, you could start by having the agency or freelancer edit a single chapter, which will give you a good idea of their capabilities and reliability in fulfilling agreements.

This chapter has highlighted how editing is likely to be the most expensive process of book production. Of course, if you're lucky enough to have a traditional publisher wanting to publish your book, then they will handle the entire process for you. However, if you choose to be a self-published author, then the whole production of the book is your responsibility. Whichever route to publication you finally choose, remember—your aim as an author is to ensure that your reader experiences an excellent quality product. That way, they'll come back for more!

CHAPTER 12

Common Grammatical Errors

Grammar is a set of English language rules that makes communication effective. The reason we write in grammatically correct language is to clearly convey our intended meaning. The purpose of grammar is to ensure readability and better communication.

I'm now going to list some of the most basic errors I see in everyday writing. If you avoid these errors, you will eliminate about 50 percent of the most common mistakes made in daily writing. Here are examples of some of the most common grammatical errors:

Use of Punctuation

The comma, represented as , is one of the most common punctuation marks used in the English language. It is used to differentiate items that make up a list or to separate two or more different clauses within the same sentence. You shouldn't put a space before a comma. However, there is always a space after a comma.

Sometimes, people add a space both before and after a comma, which is incorrect.

Comma after "and"

Some people were taught in school never to use a comma before *and* in a sentence. However, this is incorrect: A comma is used before *and* when it is relevant.

One rule that I have learned is that a comma should be used before *and* when there is a list of more than two words used in a sentence.

For example, "I like ice cream, chocolate, and apple pie."

However, when there are only two items on the list, then no commas are needed, and it is correct to write, "I like ice cream and chocolate pie."

However, commas are also used for another important purpose—separating different types of clauses in a sentence to make the intended meaning clear.

Misusing or missing out on the comma can seriously alter the meaning of the sentence.

For example:

"Let's eat, Mom!" (correct)

"Let's eat Mom!" (incorrect)

The rule for leaving no space before a punctuation mark and a space immediately after a punctuation mark also holds true for the following punctuation marks:

Full Stop (Period)

A full stop represented as . is used to end a sentence. There is no space in front of a period.

Exclamation Mark

An exclamation mark is represented as ! and is used to represent strong emotions, like excitement, anger, surprise, or anguish. The correct position for the exclamation mark is at the end of a sentence. There is no space before an exclamation mark, as it denotes the end of the sentence.

Examples include:

"Oh boy! It's so hot."

"There's no way I'm working overtime today!"

In both the sentences above, the exclamation indicates the speaker's strong emotions. Punctuation marks are there to convey your intended meaning to the reader. When we speak, we use voice modulation to convey our message. If we are angry, our tone reflects our anger and lets people know that we are angry. However, when we are writing, we don't have voice to communicate our feelings. In those instances, exclamation marks and em dashes come to our rescue.

I once had an intern who used exclamation marks excessively, which made it lose its value. Be careful with exclamation marks; use them sparingly to retain their emphasis. They are like spices in curry. Use them wisely, and your readers will fall in love with you. Excessive spice will bring tears to their eyes.

Question Mark

The question mark, represented by ? is the punctuation mark that is used to end a question. For example: "Do you want to meet at 6 pm?"

Sometimes, we write questions in fragmented sentences. At these times, a question mark is particularly useful in telling readers that it is a question and not an exclamation. For example:

"Five hours from now?"

"A million dollars?"

These fragmented sentences are sometimes used to add drama and excitement to an otherwise dull prose and is often used in a dialogue between two people.

Ellipsis

The ellipsis is represented by three dots ... which are really full stops or periods. Its usage is sometimes confusing to understand, but authors generally use it to express unfinished thoughts in a sentence. Some style guides recommend using four dots at the end of such a sentence. I always use three dots, but it's not uncommon to see writers using two dots or even five. Many are not aware that an ellipsis has three dots.

For example:
"There may be ice cream and chocolate pie to eat, but we're not sure..."

Or, it can even be used when the author has omitted a word.
"What do you...I mean, how could you?"

Other Punctuation Marks

Quotations marks are represented as " to open a speech and " to close it when the speaker has finished talking. The same applies when you start a sentence where you are quoting someone.

For example:
Robert said, "The sun is round."

As you can see, the opening quotation mark appears at the beginning of Robert's speech, and the corresponding closing quotation mark is the end. In American English, punctuation marks, like the comma and full stop, are always inside the quotation marks.

Apostrophe

The apostrophe is represented by ' and is used for multiple purposes. It can be used to show possession of something:

For example:

"It is my dad's house."

"It is the dog's bone."

In both sentences, we are using an apostrophe to show that the house or bone belongs to someone.

Or, it can be used as a contraction. Instead of writing *it is*, we could just write *it's*.

For example:

"It is a rainy day."

"It's a rainy day."

Both sentences are correct. The first sentence is more formal, while the second is less so.

Em Dash, en Dash, and Hyphen

Despite working as a professional content writer, I found that I did not know the difference between an em dash, en dash, and a hyphen. I used a hyphen in most situations, not knowing that there is a difference between the three. Neither the em dash or the en dash appear on any keyboard. That's because both symbols need to be inserted by clicking the Insert tab on the toolbar in Microsoft Word.

Here are the three symbols placed one below the other. Let's see if you can spot the difference.

-

—

–

Do you see the difference? The hyphen is the shortest among the three dashes. Hyphens are used to join two words, parts of words, and sometimes used to join an adjective with a word.

Words like part-time, one-third, president-elect, London-based are hyphenated words. Using hyphens can be confusing because there are times when certain words are hyphenated, and sometimes when they aren't. That's the irony of the English language. If you're not sure, it's always best to check. Incidentally, there is no need to insert a space before or after a hyphen.

The second of the dashes from the list above is the em dash. It is bigger than both the hyphen and the en dash. It is sometimes used instead of a comma where the writer wants to convey a strong message that needs more than just a comma. Or, it is used to add additional information. Some style guides suggest adding a space before and after an em dash, but many others suggest the opposite. I generally do not add a space either before or after an em dash.

For example:

"I met my role models—Richard, Bill, and Warren—on my flight to Amsterdam."

Imagine if we wrote these words with a comma rather than an em dash. How would it look?

"I met my role models, Richard, Bill, and Warren, on my flight to Amsterdam."

You can see that there are too many commas in this sentence, making it look rather untidy. Using an em dash, as in the earlier example, emphasizes the subjects and removes the cluttering commas. It conveys the meaning that the three people mentioned are important to the author.

The em dash is also used to add additional information to a sentence.

For example:

"I finally bought my dream car—the Ford Mustang Classic."

British vs. American English

If grammar doesn't complicate the English language enough, then we also have American English and British English to deal with. Both are English, but each has a slightly different set of rules.

In American English, *learnt* becomes *learned*. *Honour* becomes *honor*. *Colour* becomes *color*. There are many spelling differences and punctuation differences between American English and British English. I mostly write in American English. Depending on the country and your audience, you can either choose to write in American English or British English. But whichever version of English you choose, be consistent. Don't mix up the two in your book.

Bulleted Lists

When writing non-fiction, it is common to use bullet points. Bullet points are represented by a dot, tick, or square in front of the text.
The purpose of a bullet point is to:
1. Make content readable
2. Break uniformity
3. Highlight information in a lengthy document

Some common questions about using bullet points are:
- Do you start a bullet point with a capital letter?
- Do you end it with a punctuation mark?

These questions can be confusing to writers. Let me try to ease your confusion. If your bullet point is a complete sentence, then it starts with a capital letter and ends with a punctuation mark.
For example:
The benefits of working out are:
- It increases your blood circulation.
- It increases your stamina so that you can work longer hours.
- Your ability to enjoy life increases with the release of endorphins.

If you observe, the sentences above start with a capital letter and end with a full stop/period.

However, if the sentence is fragmented, then you don't need to start it with a capital letter or end it with a punctuation mark; it's a matter of choice. My advice is to be consistent with capitalization and punctuation of your bullet points. If you start one bullet point with a capital letter, then start all of them with a capital letter and vice versa.

For example:
The benefits of working out include:
- Increased blood circulation
- Increased stamina
- Ability to enjoy life

All three sentences after the bullet point are fragmented, so there is no need for punctuation.

However, the example below that misses out capital letters at the start of each point is also correct.

The benefits of working out include:
- increased blood circulation
- increased stamina
- ability to enjoy life

One of the easiest tricks to developing a good writing style is to be consistent.

Who vs. That

Two of the most commonly used words in the English language are *Who* and *That*. Do you say, a leader *that* is decisive? Or a leader *who* is decisive? It might seem like common sense, but this error is common even among professional writers. The general rule is *who* is used for people, and *that* is used for things. But it's not always as straightforward. There are instances where *that* can be used for people, as well.

Compare these sentences:
The girl who got away.

The girl that got away.
The one that got away.
Which one do you think is correct?

Strict grammarians will conclude that the correct answer is *the girl who got away*—because *who* is used for people and *that* is used for things. However, others think *that* sounds more natural. If you want to adhere strictly to grammar, then *who* is correct in this instance. However, rules can be broken if you think it makes your communication more effective. But to break the rules, you've first got to know them.

Sometimes, when we talk about a person in contempt, then *that* is often used, rather than *who*.

Adding Article A, An, The

In the English language, articles are used before nouns. A noun represents a place, person, or thing.
Examples:
Place: Beauty parlor, road, building
Person: Doctor, artist, entrepreneur
Thing: bottle, knife, car

When Do You Use A, An, and The?

A is used for something that is not specific.
Example: "I used a knife to open Robert's bottle."

In this case, we've used *a* because we are not referring to a specific knife. We are referring to just about any knife, not a particular knife.

When Do We Use *An*?

An is used instead of *a* for words that start with a vowel. Vowels are words that begin with a, e, i, o, and u. But there are exceptions to this rule. Grammarians mention that *a* or *an* is used based on pronunciation rather than the beginning letter of the word. Words that begin with a vowel sound use *an* as their article. We generally say *an hour* rather than *a hour* because the pronunciation begins with a vowel sound. So, the general rule is to use *an* instead of *a* for words whose pronunciations begin with a vowel. Focus on the sound of the beginning letter rather than its spelling.

When to Use In, On, Of, At, and About (Prepositions)

We use prepositions to connect words in a sentence. Words such as *in, on, of, at, for,* and *about* are prepositions. It is common to get confused between *in, at,* and *on*. We use *in* when we refer to something inside something else.

For example:

John lives in the city.

Here we are referring to John, who lives inside the city.

Another example:

John lives at 22, Staten Island Road.

At here refers to a specific address and not merely 'inside the city.'

Explore this sentence:

John lives on planet Earth.

The sentence suggests John lives on the surface of the planet rather than inside it.

The use of prepositions can be confusing. However, with practice and the help of a coach, you can master it quickly.

How Is a Sentence Constructed?

A sentence is a combination of words that help the author convey a complete meaning. It contains a noun or pronoun, a verb, adverb, adjectives, and a predicate. Sentences can also be divided into simple sentences, compound sentences, and complex sentences. A simple sentence generally has just one meaning. A compound sentence is typically a combination of several sentences—with the conjunctions *but, and,* and *or* used to combine two clauses or two different meanings.

Compound sentences are a combination of several ideas that are contained in clauses, which represents a main idea known as an independent clause, and a secondary idea called subordinate clauses. An independent clause can stand by itself as a full sentence, whereas a subordinate clause cannot. It is dependent for meaning on another clause, usually the main or independent clause within the sentence.

Grammar is an integral part of the English language. I've only scratched the surface and covered a few of the common grammatical errors I've seen. I haven't gone into great detail here because it can take an entire book to cover this subject. If you think you need help with grammar, I suggest you take an online course. It can be an excellent investment, even if you don't write a book, as good communication can open doors in both business and social worlds.

CHAPTER 13

Miscellaneous Pages in Your Book

WHENEVER WE OPEN A book to read, we usually find several different pages both at the beginning and, sometimes, at the end of the book. These vary from book to book, so let's have a look at a few and see the other pages they contain besides the chapters.

Most of the books have a title page, copyright information, a Table of Contents, and some have a dedication page. Many include a foreword, a preface, an introduction, sometimes a chronology, while some also contain an index.

You may be unsure of the exact purpose of some of these pages and think that you won't need them for your book but let me explain each of them.

Pages Usually Found at the Beginning of a Book

Title Page

The title page is just that—it sets out in large type the title of the book, followed by the author's name. In most non-fiction books, the title page is generally printed in black and white. If you are going to self-publish your book, you'll probably need a typesetter to help you take care of this. However, if you have a publisher, they should do this for you, so you won't have to worry about it.

Copyright Information Page

If you're a self-published author, you'll need to include a page showing copyright information about your book. This consists of the copyright symbol, author name, the name of your organization or imprint, and your business address. You can learn more about this in my book on self-publishing, where I've covered it in detail.

Table of Contents (TOC)

Most books have a TOC of some sort, as it provides help for readers when navigating the content. A simple way to insert a Table of contents for a Word document is by clicking on "References" on the Word menu bar, then clicking on "Insert table of contents." This will automatically insert a TOC, provided the title of each chapter is formatted as a heading.

If you're using a professional typesetter, I suggest asking them to add a table of contents for you rather than messing around in Word yourself. If your book is going to be published in the traditional way, then your publisher will probably arrange to have one added, so there's no need to do it yourself.

Foreword

Someone other than the author of the book, often a famous or well-known expert in the industry, usually writes the foreword. The purpose of a foreword is to introduce the author to the world. A foreword is a marketing tool more than anything else, as it's an endorsement by an expert, and is designed to add credibility to the author.

Does every book need a foreword? No, sometimes they're unnecessary. Lots of books, even bestselling ones, don't have forewords. But, if you do decide to go with a foreword, then you should approach someone who you respect and admire.

Think back to the time when you were in the research phase of writing your book, when, hopefully, you made an effort to follow my advice about connecting with important people in your industry.

One of them could make an ideal candidate to write you a foreword. But try to pick a good writer.

The last thing you need is an expert who can't write well. It could cause problems because, if you pick an expert who isn't such a great writer, you risk hurting their ego if you ultimately choose not to publish their foreword.

I recommend doing a little research first, read their blog posts, or any articles they've written to get an idea about their writing skills.

When asking someone to write a foreword for your book, make sure you make your expectations clear, but try not to be too pushy. There are really no rules as to how a foreword should be written, as long as it's well-written and enhances the credibility of the author. Ideally, it should aim to persuade the reader to read the rest of the book. As mentioned earlier, the foreword is a marketing tool and should be treated as such, in order to benefit you in promoting your book.

Imagine if you wrote a book on computing—with a foreword by Bill Gates. The sensible author would mention this on the front cover of the book, as it would dramatically enhance the book's credibility.

Use the foreword wisely if you choose to include one. However, there's no need to add one just for the heck of it. As you start writing your book, remember to keep an eye open for any potential candidates to write an excellent foreword for your book.

Prologue

When I think about books with prologues, two spring to mind—one is Richard Branson's Autobiography *Losing My Virginity*, the other is Peter Lynch's book *One Up on Wall Street*. The authors talk about incidents that happened on specific days of their lives. This serves to set a nice tone and mood for the chapters that follow.

For instance, Lynch narrates incidents that happened on Oct 16, 1987, and how they shaped his thinking going forward, as well as the lessons he took from them. In these cases, the prologues help set readers' expectations for the rest of the book. If you believe that a background story could benefit your readers, then a prologue could make an interesting addition.

Preface

An author's relationship with her readers starts from the moment the reader picks up a book. Some writers capitalize on this by including a preface at the start of their book.

It's been said that "the game behind the game is more interesting than the game," and a preface gives authors a chance to add interest by explaining the story behind their book.

It can outline the reasons why the author chose to write the book, their motivation, and the effort put in behind the scenes to complete the book.

Acknowledgements

I remember a client of mine asking me, where in her book, she could acknowledge the contribution of her photographer. This was quite reasonable, as authors usually take several months, sometimes years, to write a book, and get help from several people along the way whose assistance they want to acknowledge.

While the acknowledgment may not matter so much to you, the people whose names are mentioned will feel special to be acknowledged for playing a role in the making of your book.

Introduction

Most people, whether online or offline, generally read the introduction before buying a book. That's the reason why your introduction should aim to encourage the reader to buy your book.

In my experience, many authors don't take the introduction seriously enough, filling it with fluff that fails to draw readers in. Some writing coaches suggest that the introduction should be kept short. I'm not sure if I agree with that advice: Introductions should be just the right length to keep your audience excited and entice readers to keep turning the pages. But what exactly should an introduction cover? Is there a template?

Let's look in more detail at putting together an outline:

THE HOOK: This should be something that catches the attention of the reader from the get-go. I've found that a personal story often works well. No two stories will be the same, but the main aim in every case should be to kick off with something attention-grabbing.

TELL THE READER WHAT'S IN IT FOR THEM: Most people are looking for something that benefits them, so give them a good reason to buy the book and keep on reading it. To achieve this, look back over the notes you made when we started out on this journey of learning together—when you wrote down the book's objectives, the reason you wrote it, and the motivation behind it. Most importantly, tell the reader how your insights will benefit them.

EXPECTATIONS: What can the reader expect from the rest of the book? This is your chance to tell the reader in a nutshell what information they can expect to find in the book and what they can learn from it that fulfills a specific need or desire they have. Keep it short and simple, but make the most of the opportunity to showcase the benefits they'll gain from your insights.

WHY YOU: Take the initiative by stamping your authority by telling the reader why you're the best person to have written it. But please be careful not to come across as though you're bragging—that can be an instant turn-off for readers—no one likes a self-obsessed bragger. In my view, the best approach is to share a personal story of challenge, charting the obstacles you overcame, the sweet taste of triumph, and the feeling of immense satisfaction you experienced as a result that you now want the reader to benefit from.

PROBLEM SOLVING: A good non-fiction book should be a solution to a reader's problem. So, tell the reader what problem you're helping them solve and the solution you are providing. I prefer not to summarize the entire book at this stage, as that can be saved for the concluding chapter of the book.

Please remember that the outline listed above is just a guideline—they're not carved in stone. If you want to do it differently, then go ahead and figure out an outline that works for you. But don't forget to take into account that the objective of the introduction is to *entice the reader to read the rest of the book.*

Pages Found at the Back of a Book

Now, let's take a look at the different types of pages that are usually found at the end of the book:

Index

Indexes have appeared as part of printed books for a long time. An index is a reference tool that gives the reader an option to go back and forth within the book to reference specific information.

Not only is an index useful, or even necessary in some circumstances, it also makes the book look more professional and well organized.

You can easily create an index for a Word document, or you can ask your editor to do it for you. Some editors might charge a small fee for providing this service, but you can learn to do it yourself—it's not as complicated as it might seem at first.

Appendix

An appendix is a place where any additional information that might be beneficial to your reader can be added. For instance, if you mention an article you've written in the body of the book, you can reproduce the article in the appendix instead of mentioning a web link. That way, the reader can turn to the appendix of the book and read the article right away rather than accessing it via a web link.

Appendices can include almost anything—articles, research reports, case studies, charts, images, and pretty much any information that doesn't fit into the body of the book. The information in the appendix should be supplemental information, perhaps concerning something you mentioned in the body of the book, but want to elaborate on, but that, if included in the chapter, might disrupt the flow of the chapter.

Although the appendix option allows you to add as much information as you want, it's important to avoid adding things that aren't relevant or supplemental to the book as a whole.

Glossary

If, in your book, you use technical terms that your audience may not immediately understand, the glossary is the place to record them and define their meaning. For example, if you write a book on finance, you might use phrases like "working capital," "margin of safety," and so on. You don't want to force your reader to guess their meaning or put down your book so that they can go and look them up online. Prevent that by adding any industry terms or jargon (if you can't avoid using it) to the glossary. The glossary is usually in alphabetical order, or sometimes there may be a sub-glossary for each chapter or section, so that the words and terms are easy to find.

Bibliography/References

A bibliography is a place to mention any references used while writing your book. It's where all the information, such as useful links to, for example, research reports, books, and any other sources used as reference or research information for your book can be listed. The correct method for citing sources in the bibliography varies from style guide to style guide, so make sure to use the appropriate one, which could be MLA, Chicago, AMA, or any other style that you've used throughout the book.

Resources

This is sometimes called "Further Reading," and is the place where you can recommend more books that might interest your reader. If you want to recommend a list of books, tools, software, or other material you feel might benefit readers, this is the section where they can be listed.

Also, there are times when authors mention tools, websites, or books they consider might be helpful to readers in the body of the book. It's always a good idea to collate and organize these into a list in the resources section.

Having reviewed all the different types of pages that can be included in books, you must decide the ones that are necessary and which can be left out. Few books contain all the pages discussed here. Whether certain pages are included or not is based on the author's preference. If you're self-publishing, you have the freedom to go against the grain and add sections that are not mentioned here, if you think they make your book more interesting.

To sum up, the purpose of this chapter is to give you, the new author, an idea of the types of pages authors can choose to use in a book and their purpose for doing so. I hope this gives you all the information necessary to decide for yourself the pages you want to include in your book. Some have little more than novelty value, while others can help promote your book, benefit the reader, and provide a great overall reading experience.

CHAPTER 14

Business Models for Nonfiction Authors

A WISE MARKETER ONCE said, "Good marketers make money at the front door, and great marketers make money at the back door."

But what does this mean for anyone wanting to make money as an author? Well, for our purposes, it means that there are several ways to make money from the business of being an author.

The Direct Method

The most obvious is the direct method of making money from actual sales of your book. For example, if you price your paperback at $10, you earn a 60% royalty on Amazon after deducting the printing costs. If the book costs $3 to print, then the total profit from the sale of each book is $6 minus $3—a total of $3.

Scale that up a little to, say, selling 1000 books a month; that would give you an income of $3000. Of course, you'll need to deduct other expenses from that figure, for example, marketing, publicity, and manpower costs, if they apply.

Besides paperbacks, royalties from the sale of eBooks can also produce a profit. eBooks can be slightly more profitable than paperbacks because there are no printing costs involved. However, this advantage is offset by the fact that eBooks are generally sold at a lower price than print books.

Rapid Release Strategy

Authors profiting from the direct publishing method use a strategy popularly called Rapid Release; this is when an author releases books frequently to cater to the reading appetite of their loyal readers.

However, this strategy comes with a big challenge. Authors need to be both good and fast writers. For instance, some authors write and publish one book a month. Therefore, the rapid release approach is unlikely to suit slower writers, but if you can write quickly and to a high standard for several hours every day, then this strategy could work for you.

Another challenge of the rapid release approach is that, as an author, you're relying on a loyal group of readers to keep on buying your books. However, the appetite of your readers could be much higher than the number of books you can produce. Therefore, one book a month is usually the norm for authors who use the rapid release strategy.

As with any skill, it takes time for a first-time author to develop their writing muscle. But while writing regularly takes a lot of discipline and energy, it gets easier the longer you keep at it. Some authors have written over 100 books in their lifetime. What would happen if you wrote 12 books a year and built an audience of 10,000 subscribers so that around 1000 of them bought every book you wrote? That would mean you'd make $3000 every month. If the number of buyers doubled, the figure would be $6000. If they tripled, that'd be a cool $9000. So, you need 3000 loyal buyers a month to cross the $100,000 mark annually.

The Indirect Method

Not sure you can realistically produce one book a month? Then, follow the alternative strategy offered by the indirect approach. This could involve anything from offering coaching/consulting services, providing information products, organizing events, and doing public speaking gigs. Authors like Brian Tracy, Tony Robbins, and Jack Canfield use the indirect model, in which the book features mainly as a publicity and lead generation tool. Events like retreats can cost upwards of $10,000. Imagine building a loyal reader base and selling a retreat for $10,000 per person; that's a cool million dollars if you sell to 100 people.

Retreats

Retreats have a broad appeal, as they involve both fun and learning. A retreat is usually a 5-day program allowing attendees not only to spend time in a peaceful location away from the city for much needed rest and relaxation, but also offers the chance for learning in a fun environment. Retreats involve both learning and entertainment activities. The value proposition of a retreat for the attendee is its similarity to a mini vacation, where learning, brainstorming and making new friends are central attractions. In addition, retreats offer essential opportunities for networking and entertainment. So, as well as learning, the audience gets an opportunity to meet people with similar interests, which can bring lifelong benefits. Some years ago, I remember attending a workshop in a retreat format, and many of the people I met there remain friends even today.

Information Products

Information products, on the other hand, can be online or downloadable courses. The advantage of a digital product is that it costs almost nothing once it's set up, yet a video course, for instance, has a higher perceived value than a book. How much can you charge your buyer for a book? $10? Maybe, $15? But clients pay upwards of $100 for an online course with videos, quizzes, and downloadable materials. Some courses can cost up to $1500. Once you create the course, the only thing needed is to handle the marketing. Everything else can be automated, enabling you to earn a passive income. If, for example, you charge $1500 per course, there's the possibility of making over a million dollars a year—and that's selling only to 667 attendees each year.

Public Speaking Opportunities

Speaking opportunities also offer authors money-making possibilities. Did you know some authors are paid anything from $10,000 to more than $100,000 for each speaking gig? In my experience, the biggest mistake authors make is not honing their public speaking skills and applying them successfully at conferences, a failure that can quickly jeopardize a speaker's career.

Public speaking is such a popular and lucrative career for today's authors that there are dedicated consultants and speaker bureaus whose sole job it is to contact authors and book them for speaking gigs. If you think public speaking could be a good avenue for you, the first step is making a video of yourself speaking, so that prospective clients can watch and be sure that you can deliver an entertaining and informative speech. A three to four-minute demo video is ideal for showcasing your skills to prospective clients.

One-On-One Coaching

One-on-one coaching is another possible revenue stream for authors. However, it won't provide you with a passive income, which means you may need to charge your clients relatively high rates compared to other revenue streams.

Live Workshops and Seminars

Live workshops and seminars are popular events that provide opportunities for authors to create additional revenue streams. For example, they are the perfect marketplace for upselling your online courses, DVDs, and even personal coaching services. Plus, your audience gets the chance to meet you in the flesh, allowing you to make a positive personal impact that's likely to boost sales of your other products.

Affiliate Marketing

Affiliate marketing is when authors are paid a referral fee for recommending a product. The business shares a unique affiliate link with a code, which, as an author, you share with your audience. Then, when a product is purchased through that affiliate link, you are paid a commission. However, this comes with a warning: it's advisable only to promote products that you trust.

Services

I help authors self-publish books by taking writers from a blank page to being a self-published author. But my services don't stop there; they also include designing the book cover, taking care of the interior design, editing, and eventually setting the book up for distribution. These are the type of comprehensive services that people learn about by reading my book. You can use your book as a marketing tool to sell your services.

Software

Selling software is another area providing money-making opportunities to authors. Don't worry if you don't have the necessary programming skills; simply hire an experienced programmer to create the software for you. For example, say you write a book about time management, creating a software product that tracks unproductive activities could be a viable source of additional revenue for you.

Membership Sites

Establishing a membership site is an alternative way to create a revenue stream. A big advantage of membership sites is their ability to provide authors with a recurring income. It works like this: You build a community where your readers subscribe to be members of your online platform, which can include a social network where members build a friends' lists and message each other. The platform might offer members access to forums where they get help with their writing skills or help others with theirs. Readers get access to a community that shares, cares, and is a source of mutual support for its members.

It's not always practical to exploit all the many possibilities for creating revenue, but potential authors can cherry-pick those most suited to their skills and are the easiest to implement.

Checklist

Here's a simple checklist to keep in mind when choosing your revenue streams:

#1 Skill

Which revenue stream is most compatible with your skills? For instance, are you are a fast writer who can churn out books quickly? Then adopting a rapid release strategy might work best for you.

You're a good writer, but you average just one book a year. That's unlikely to satisfy the appetite of your audience. But maybe you're a great organizer, able to create events on-the-go, people love your personality, and you enjoy organizing events. If this is you, then organizing retreats could be the way to go. However, it's important to remember that this is a long-haul project requiring dedication and patience, as building up a retreat that people love and admire, and that wins a loyal fanbase, takes a long time.

The ultimate aim of any retreat business is to become a flagship event that people visit every year. However, there are many vital operational issues, such as obtaining the correct insurance and complying with relevant regulations, which can be time-consuming and expensive to implement. It's like running an event management company. You need salespeople to follow up and ensure sales are completed, volunteers and staff to welcome guests at the hotel, as well as someone to source and book talent, including entertainment and workshop instructors, to help create content for the event. As you can see, setting up a retreat can be a daunting task.

Upgrading Your Skills

But what if you don't have the skills to leverage any of the revenue streams highlighted here? The simple answer is that you'll need to learn them. At this point, you must ask yourself some hard questions as to whether this is a realistic goal for you. Is training available, where, and at what cost? How long will it take, and how steep is the learning curve? If it's steep and learning is likely to be time-consuming and expensive, is it worth undertaking? If your business plan is long-term, you may decide it's worth going ahead. If not, it's wise to consider alternative, more practical, or affordable ways to grow your business.

#2 Goals

What are your goals? Every author has different goals. Some authors only have a story to tell, so making an income from their writing isn't a priority for them. These authors may have full-time jobs or run successful businesses, and only want to share their story and write for the sheer joy of it.

Alternatively, others write as an income-producing hobby. For instance, I have a friend whose goal is to learn a new skill every year. Her main role is as a homemaker, but she would like to develop a side business writing from home.

#3 Readers and Their Needs

In the final reckoning, it's our readers that we're catering to. That poses several questions: What do our readers want and need? What sort of content do they respond best to? Are they interested in membership sites, retreats, in-person workshops, or online courses? What topics and themes are they most interested in?

Readers fall into several categories. For instance, some readers are introverts only interested in reading books and aren't interested in attending offline events, preferring to stay at home. More sociable readers may be inclined to attend retreats because their major interest is making lifelong friendships with likeminded people.

An effective and inexpensive way of finding out readers' interests is by asking them to complete a survey. Bear in mind, though, that outcomes from surveys aren't always an accurate reflection of what readers want, as they often don't know that themselves—after all, you're essentially asking them to imagine something that doesn't exist. Nevertheless, surveys can provide vital insights into readers' preferences and their appetite for certain activities. In the past, I have been surprised by survey results. It's easy to organize a survey if you already have a list—simply sign up on SurveyMonkey, or a similar site, design a survey, and then send it out to everyone on your list.

The revenue streams highlighted here only come into play once authors have built a loyal audience. Along with writing a book, an indie author's job is also to build a loyal readership.

CHAPTER 15

Options for Non-Writers

IN 2004, PARIS HILTON, the socialite and hotel heiress, released her first book, Confessions of an Heiress: A Tongue-in-Chic Peek Behind the Pose. At first glance, Hilton doesn't seem the writing type, but who knows? Perhaps she had always wanted to write and, while she hasn't yet set the world alight with her literary offerings, she may yet surprise us all.

On entering any modern bookstore, you'll see books penned by the rich and famous—celebrities, actors, politicians, and entrepreneurs, among other luminaries, have all made their contributions to the bookshelves. But how many of the words in those books were actually penned by the authors themselves? One can't help but suspect that, in many cases, the services of a professional ghostwriter may have been used.

Few people openly admit to using ghostwriters to help them pen their books. Ghostwriters usually have to agree to signing NDAs (Non-disclosure agreements), which bar them from revealing that they ghostwrote a book. If any credit is given to the ghostwriter at all, then the words "co-author" or "collaborator" might be used.

Some celebrities have claimed that they wrote every word in their book, only to be embarrassingly contradicted by publishers and frenemies. So, we must ask ourselves the question as to why celebrities and influential people who want to write a book enlist the help of a ghostwriter.

Celebrities, sportspeople, and politicians, to name a few, often have great stories to tell, stories that people want to read. And, although they might want to pen their autobiography someday, they may lack the necessary skills to write a book.

Anyone who has written a book knows that writing is hard work. It requires skill, ability, and practice. It's like running marathons, where it takes time and persistence to develop stamina. For instance, it can take over 200 hours to write a book, yet the skill of the celebrity or professional probably lies elsewhere than in writing. For example, a doctor who earns $350 an hour might be better off spending their time saving lives, a skill they've perfected over many years of practice, rather than writing a book.

What Is Ghostwriting?

Ghostwriting is when the author of the book hasn't written the book, but someone else has written it on their behalf. For example, let's say Ted Sorensen writes a book on behalf of John F. Kennedy, and Kennedy publishes the book with his name as the author. That makes Sorenson the ghostwriter, while Kennedy is named as author, although, technically, he didn't actually write the book.

Here's another question: Is ghostwriting ethical? What if all the words were Kennedy's? He just told the story to his ghostwriter, and the ghostwriter penned it for him. Looked at that way, you could say that it's rather like dictating your story to a friend, who then writes it down for you.

It's still essentially the author's story (and content), irrespective of who arranges it into words on the page for them.

Ghostwriting is about transferring information from one form to another. The author communicates the information orally to the ghostwriter, who records it, puts it into a book, organizes the content, and tweaks the language to make it reader friendly.

The place where ghostwriting gets murky is when the information in the book comes from the ghostwriter and not the author. That sort of ghostwriting can be deceptive to the reader.

Should You or Should You Not Use a Ghostwriter?

Whether or not to use a ghostwriter is a personal decision. I'd prefer authors to develop their writing skills, and write not just one, but several books. But I also understand that many people may not want to go through the tedious process of writing their own books—after all, it's very hard work! They prefer instead to hire a ghostwriter, who doesn't just write the book for them, but also acts as a guide and coach in the process of getting their story written and published.

However, cost is an important factor to consider in deciding if you want to go down the ghostwriting route. For example, a typical ghostwriting project can cost anywhere between $15,000 to $30,000, and there may be little return on that investment. It's a sad fact that most books don't make back the money they cost to produce. In fact, unless it's a personal branding exercise, I don't see how people can recover the money they spend on a ghostwritten book.

Still, it's true that, sometimes, people are driven to publish books for reasons of vanity. Or, at other times, are desperate to share their message and their legacy, whatever the cost.

I did a ghostwriting project for a client of mine. He created a PowerPoint presentation and recorded his voice in the background. I had his voice transcribed and rewrote the entire content, organized it into chapters, and then self-published the book on his behalf. The project benefited his business because he could now give away something tangible during his seminar for attendees to take away.

How to Hire a Ghostwriter?

Good ghostwriters are worth their weight in gold. They can take your story, polish it, and make it enjoyable for the reader. You could be spending a lot of time with a ghostwriter, so its best to pick someone you like, admire, and respect. A good ghostwriter will help you reveal more about yourself. They should be inquisitive, curious, and genuinely want to know more about you.

In addition, past experience does matter in this case. If the ghostwriter has done similar projects before, then they're likely to have a good understanding of the whole process and, therefore, be better able to avoid rookie mistakes. But, just like anything in life, experience doesn't always equal expertise, and it's hard to tell if someone is good until you work with them. Professionals are expensive, and one can only find out how good they are after a sizable amount of money has been spent. Finding a good ghostwriter is both a skill and an art, that's why a good question to ask your potential ghostwriter is whether or not they have a process.

Here's how the process in our company works:

Step 1: Decide the Topic of the Book

Most people already have a topic in mind when they set out to publish a book, which is usually related to their field of work. Some people may be looking to write down their family history; they take pride in their family and want to document it for the world to read, as well as for future generations.

Step 2: Choose a Title for the Book

The title is one of the hardest things to come up with. One advantage of hiring a ghostwriter is that they can brainstorm and usually come up with a few good titles to help the author out.

Step 3: Interview

Once the title of the book is confirmed and an initial "get to know" session is carried out, we set up a more detailed interview with the client, where we ask in-depth questions related to the content of the book. The ultimate purpose of this interview is to come up with a list of chapters.

Step 4: Prepare an Outline with a List of Chapters

Once we've had a detailed interview with the client, we prepare a list of chapters. We send the list of chapters to the client, which they either approve or send back to us with feedback and changes. Once approved by the client, we move to the next step.

Step 5: Second Interview

We do another round of interviews with the client, where we go into much more detail than the first one. We try to "knock out" each chapter from the client and get most of the content for the book from this interview.

Step 6: Transcribing

Once the interview is done, a transcriber transcribes the interview.

Step 7: Preparing Chapters

The transcribed interview will then be converted into chapters. Once it's turned into chapters, one of our writers will rewrite the entire book into a book format.

Step 8: Editing

Once the manuscript is ready, our editors will do line-editing and copy-editing, which involves reconstructing sentences to improve style, flow, grammar, and punctuation.

Step 9: Proofreading

A proofreader will go through the entire book, checking for spelling and grammatical errors.

Step 10: Finishing Touches

The finishing touches will be done to the book by adding the foreword, preface, and acknowledgments, if necessary.

Step 11: Cover Designing

A book cover is designed and sent to the client for approval.

Step 12: Distribution

Once the book is ready, we acquire ISBNs and set it up for worldwide distribution.

A process that can make ghostwriting easier and faster is to prepare a PowerPoint presentation and record the presentation as if you're speaking to an audience. Then, you can get someone to transcribe the presentation for you. The transcriber will convert your voice to text, after which you can get someone to rewrite, edit, and proofread the text.

Ghostwriting is a long, elaborate, and intensive process, which takes time, effort, and talent. As already mentioned, professionals cost money, and good talent doesn't come cheap. So, if you're planning on using professionals, be prepared to spend anywhere between $15,000 to $30,000 before your book is ready for publication. It's your call as to whether it's worth paying that kind of money to get a book written.

If you don't want to spend that kind of money, the other option is to roll up your sleeves and write the book yourself, which involves lots of hours of learning and practice. There's always going to be a learning curve that will take time and effort to climb. Initially, you will undoubtedly find the process hard, but, as you keep doing it, it gets easier. I can personally attest to the fact that, while practice may not make you perfect, it will make you better.

As a twist on the PowerPoint presentation option mentioned earlier, you can also use dictation software and speak directly into it. *Dragon Dictate* is a popular example of this kind of software. Authors who use dictation software mostly follow a rapid release strategy. This means they're getting books published quickly for an audience with a healthy appetite for reading.

While the average person speaks at 120 to 160 words per minute, I doubt if many people can type at this speed. However, dictation software could be the answer for you, as it's an effective way to speed up your publishing process, especially if you don't want to write. At a rough estimate, if you speak for 60 minutes, you'll end up with around 7200 words of text. If your target is 60,000 words, that's approximately 8 hours of speaking. Now, compare that to 200 hours of writing—it's obvious how much faster and easier using dictation technology can be. Users say that it takes a while to get used to it. Like a lot of voice recognition technology, it can be inaccurate, but I'm told that the software gets used to your voice over time, and the accuracy improves.

There's no doubt that writing is a difficult skill, which explains why there have been so many attempts over the years to find ways to alleviate the pain of writing a book. Non-writers, especially people who have been in professions where they've rarely needed to write, often find writing to be an arduous task. On the other hand, if you're a "glass half full" type of person, you'll realize it's not really that difficult. Yes, it requires practice, persistence, and discipline, but there's lots of help out there. For instance, you might consider taking a writing course, joining your local writer's circle, taking a class in grammar, and, of course, read books on the subject—like this one. The learning curve might be longer for some than others, but practice and the right guidance will get you there.

So, let's sum up: If you're a non-writer, depending on your priorities, there are several options out there to help you get published. You can decide to invest in some good dictation software, hire a ghostwriter, or brave the learning curve and write a book the old-fashioned way, as authors have been doing successfully for centuries.

You need to evaluate your options and find a process that works for you—many authors out there use innovative methods to get their books produced quickly. Remember, there's more than one way to write a book, and the only way to find out what is going to work for you in the long-term is to be prepared for a little trial and error.

In the next chapter, we summarize everything that you've learned up until now and give you some final tips for completing your manuscript.

Closing Thoughts

I HOPE YOU'VE ENJOYED reading this book as much as I've enjoyed putting it together. You may have already guessed that one of the reasons I wrote this book is because people keep telling me how much they want to write a book, yet, when I meet them several years later, I find that it's still just an idea. I'd like to see more of these ideas transformed into great books.

We've already established that good writing skills matter, but persistence and discipline are even more important—without them, no book will be finished. Here are some final tips to get you motivated:

#1 Make a Start

It may seem obvious, but to finish writing your book, you must first begin. That means, getting down to typing words into your word processor or putting pen to paper.

#2 Discipline

We discussed how the simple act of setting aside a specific time of the day just for writing instills discipline and keeps you going even on days when you don't feel quite so excited about it. Some days, the words will flow smoothly, but there will be days when writing will be a struggle. But take courage. Just follow my advice about establishing a habit of writing every day at a regular time. It will ensure that irrespective of your feeling, you'll continue to move forward.

#3 Book Plan

We've covered how planning your work can save you time and keep you organized. The book plan is one of the most important building blocks in the whole book writing process. So, start your book with a plan.

#4 Create a List of Chapters

Remember, we discussed how a book plan has an objective? Each chapter is a step forward on the path that leads the reader towards achieving the main objective of the book, which is why they bought it in the first place.

#5 Create a Chapter Outline

Creating an outline breaks up what could be a large chapter that contains a lot of information into smaller and more manageable parts. While chapter outlines can be changed as you go along, having that basic outline to return to will always provide that bedrock of direction and focus.

#6 Learn to Self-Edit

We also discussed how self-editing is an integral part of the writing process. Trying to make as good a job as possible of polishing your work before you send it to a professional editor can help you improve the final quality of your manuscript.

#7 Hiring a Professional Editor

Although editing can be expensive, having that professional touch can make a remarkable difference to your finished product. I like to compare good editors to good tailors—just as a tailor's attention to detail can enhance your look, an editor's little changes, however small they might seem, can make your writing more reader-friendly.

#6 Perfectionism

All you perfectionists out there, try to remember that a good book doesn't need to be perfect. It only needs to be good enough to be published. If you are 90% satisfied, it's still good enough to go to print. The hardest part for a writer is to say, "I am done!" It's natural for writers to want to continuously make tweaks to their work, worrying if their audience will accept them or not. But, if you've done your best to meet readers' expectations, then try not to worry too much. Chances are they won't be able to tell good enough from perfect anyway!

I wouldn't like to end this book by saying, "Our delightful journey together has come to an end." I would rather say, "Our journey has just begun."

I wish you all the best in your writing journey. Don't forget, you can keep in touch with me by subscribing to my newsletter at www.authormag.com/firstbook

Bibliography

Agnihotri, Neeraj. *Procrasdemon: The Artist's Guide To LIberation From Procrastination. Amazon*. Accessed June 1, 2020. https://www.amazon.com/Procrasdemon-Artists-Guide-LIberation-Procrastination-ebook/dp/B07SG5VGGY/.

Breus, Michael. *The Power of When: Learn the Best Time to Do Everything*. London, UK: Vermilion, 2016.

Clark, Thomas. "174 Tips From Bestselling Writers." *Writer's Digest*, September 1986.

Currey, Mason. *Daily Rituals: How Great Minds Make Time, Find Inspiration, and Get to Work*. Picador; Main Market Ed. edition, 2014.

Field, Syd. *Screenplay: the Basics of Film Writing*. New York, NY: Delacorte Press, 1979.

Godin, Seth. "Streaks." Seth's Blog, August 7, 2019. https://seths.blog/2019/08/streaks/.

Government Digital Service. "How Copyright Protects Your Work." GOV.UK. GOV.UK, November 18, 2015. https://www.gov.uk/copyright.

A Hand Book of Copyright Law. Accessed June 1, 2020. http://copyright.gov.in/documents/handbook.html.

Huntress, Caelan. "My Favourite Quote of All Time Is a Misattribution." Medium. Mission.org, August 25, 2017. https://medium.com/the-mission/my-favourite-quote-of-all-time-is-a-misattribution-66356f22843d.

King, Stephen. *On Writing: a Memoir of the Craft*. New York, NY: Scribner, 2010.

Lombardi, Vincent T. "What It Takes to Be Number One." What It Takes to be Number One | Vince Lombardi. Accessed June 1, 2020. http://www.vincelombardi.com/number-one.html.

"Plagiarize." Merriam-Webster. Merriam-Webster. Accessed June 1, 2020. https://www.merriam-webster.com/dictionary/plagiarize.

"PROCESS: Meaning in the Cambridge English Dictionary." Cambridge Dictionary. Accessed June 1, 2020. https://dictionary.cambridge.org/dictionary/english/process.

Quiller-Couch, Arthur Thomas. *On the Art of Writing*. Mineola, NY: Dover Publications, 2006.

"Research." Merriam-Webster. Merriam-Webster. Accessed June 1, 2020. https://www.merriam-webster.com/dictionary/research.

Rowe, Kenneth Thorpe. *Write That Play*. New York, NY: Funk and Wagnalls, 1968.

Schlesinger, Jill. "Another Great One-Liner from Warren Buffett." CBS News. CBS Interactive, November 4, 2009. https://www.cbsnews.com/news/another-great-one-liner-from-warren-buffett-03-11-2009/.

"STORY: Meaning in the Cambridge English Dictionary." Cambridge Dictionary. Accessed June 1, 2020. https://dictionary.cambridge.org/dictionary/english/story.

Stuart, Debra. "Khaled Hosseini." Khaled Hosseini | The Story Mint, 2012. https://www.thestorymint.com/content/khaled-hosseini.

United States Copyright Office. Ideas, Methods, or Systems, Ideas, Methods, or Systems § (2012).

Zinsser, William Knowlton. *On Writing Well: The Classic Guide to Writing Nonfiction*. New York, NY: Collins Reference, 2005.

Index

A

accidental plagiarism, 46
acknowledgments, 119
affiliate marketing, 129
Agnihotri, Neeraj, 22
Amazon, 7
American English, 109
anthologies, 20
apostrophe, 107
appendix, 121
Aristotle, 21, 56

B

basal ganglia, 23
before-after-bridge, 59
bibliography, 122
book plan, 38
Branson, Richard, 118
British English, 109
bullet points, 109
business and work memoir, 18

C

Campbell, Joseph, 60
celebrities, 136
celebrity memoir, 16
chapter hook, 78
Chicago Manual of Style, 48
climax, 58
comma, 103
confessional memoir, 15
copy editing, 82
copy editor, 82
copyright information, 116
copyright laws, 52
copyright works in the UK, 51
copyrights, 50
Copyscape, 49
Covey, Stephen, 6
Crichton, Michael, 80

D

definition of process, 73
developmental editing, 81
discipline, 2
Durant, Will, 21

E

ellipsis, 106
em dash, 107
en dash, 108
exclamation mark, 105

F

fact-checking, 82
family memoir, 18
Ferris, Tim, 31
fiction writers, 57
Field, Syd, 56
first draft, 79
fitness memoirs, 19
food memoirs, 17
foreword, 117
full stop, 104

G

ghostwriters, 135
glossary, 122
Godin, Seth, 24
Goins, Jeff, 9

grammar, 103

H

habits, 23
habits of successful authors, 22
HARO, 81
Hemingway, Ernest, 24
hero's journey, 60
Hilton, Paris, 135
Hosseini, Khaled, 26
human brain, 23
humorous memoirs, 17
hyphen, 107

I

income from royalties, 8
information products, 128
inspirational memoirs, 14
introduction page, 119

K

King, Stephen, 87
Kingsolver, Barbara, 25

L

L'Engle, Madeleine, 2
length of your book, 40
list of Chapters, 42
live workshops, 129

M

make money simply by selling books, 7
marketable title, 30
memoirs, 13
monomyth, 60
Morrison, Toni, 2
mosaic' plagiarism, 48

N

nostalgia memoir, 14

O

objective of the book, 38
one-on-one coaching, 129
outlining, 74

P

parenting memoirs, 19
period, 104
plagiarism, 46
plagiarism check, 92
planning, 37
political memoir, 16
position themselves as authorities, 6
pre-climax, 58
preface, 118
primary research, 67
proofreading, 82
public domain content, 51
purpose for writing, 38

Q

question mark, 105
quotations marks, 106

R

Ramayana, 60
rapid release strategy, 126
reader's problem, 40
relationship memoirs, 17
research, 66
resources, 122
Rowe, Kenneth, 56

S

schedule, 79
secondary research, 67
self-editing, 86
self-help books, 13
selling software, 130
Shakespeare, 56
social currency, 5
speaking opportunities, 128
sports memoirs, 16
storytelling, 53

T

table of contents, 116
target audience, 39
the three-act structure, 56
title of a book, 29
title of the book, 38
title page, 116

Tracy, Brian, 6
traditional publishers, 5
travel memoir, 15
types of nonfiction books, 13
types of plagiarism, 47

U

US copyright law, 52

V

vanity publishing, 5
Vishwanath, Kaavya, 45
Volger, Christopher, 61

Z

Zissner, William, 80

ABOUT THE AUTHOR

Vinil Ramdev has helped several authors publish their books. His life accidents include authoring books, starting businesses in retail, events, publishing, and serving a sentence as managing editor of a print magazine.

Connect with him on:
Facebook: https://www.facebook.com/vinilr/
LinkedIn: https://www.linkedin.com/in/vinilramdev/
Twitter: https://twitter.com/vinilramdev
Newsletter: https://www.authormag.com/firstbook
Email: vinil@publishedge.com

PUBLISHING SERVICES

PublishEdge is a one stop solution for all your self-publishing needs.

Our services include:
- Editing
- Typesetting
- Cover Design
- Ghostwriting
- Distribution
- Author Websites

To avail our services, please visit www.publishedge.com

www.ingramcontent.com/pod-product-compliance
Lightning Source LLC
Chambersburg PA
CBHW012207090526
44583CB00022BA/2938